ESSENTIALS OF
PSYCHOANALYSIS

BRUNNER/MAZEL
BASIC PRINCIPLES INTO PRACTICE SERIES
Series Editor: Natalie H. Gilman

The *Brunner/Mazel Basic Principles Into Practice Series* is designed to present—in a series of concisely written, easily understandable volumes—the basic theory and clinical principles associated with a variety of disciplines and types of therapy. These volumes will serve not only as "refreshers" for practicing therapists, but also as basic texts on the college and graduate level.

BRUNNER/MAZEL
BASIC PRINCIPLES INTO PRACTICE SERIES
VOLUME 2

ESSENTIALS OF PSYCHOANALYSIS

HERBERT S. STREAN, D.S.W.

BRUNNER/MAZEL *Publishers* • NEW YORK

Library of Congress Cataloging-in-Publication Data
Strean, Herbert S.
   Essentials of psychoanalysis / Herbert S. Strean.
       p.   cm.— (Brunner/Mazel basic principles into practice
series; v.2)
   Includes bibliographical references and index
   ISBN 0-87630-737-3
   1. Psychoanalysis I. Title. II. Series: Brunner/Mazel basic
principles into practice library; v.2.
RC504.S79 1994
616.89'17—dc20

                                94-2891
                                CIP

Published by
BRUNNER/MAZEL, INC.
19 Union Square West
New York, New York 10003

Manufactured in the United States of America
10 9 8 7 6 5 4 3 2 1

To the Candidates and Faculty,
present and past,
of the
New York Center for Psychoanalytic Training

In Friendship.

CONTENTS

PREFACE

No perspective on human behavior is as complex, controversial, and misunderstood as psychoanalysis. Ever since Freud introduced psychoanalysis to the world close to a century ago, psychoanalysis as a theory of human personality, a perspective on maladaptive functioning, a treatment technique, and a method of research has been adored and abhorred, lauded and vilified, heavily used and frequently abused by both mental health professionals and nonprofessionals.

Although there are literally thousands of books and articles available to the psychotherapist on various aspects of psychoanalysis as an orientation that deals with human functioning and its treatment, there is virtually no one book on the market that specifically focuses on the main essentials of psychoanalytic theory and treatment. This book is written to fill this gap in the psychotherapeutic literature.

Regardless of the mental health practitioner's unit of diagnostic attention, his or her theoretical predilections, or his or her preferred therapeutic modality, it is the thesis of this text that all psychotherapists can profitably utilize several psychoanalytic concepts in their assessment of patients and their treatment of them. For example, whether the practitioner is working with individuals, dyads, families, or groups, and regardless of the setting in which he or she practices, every mental health professional should understand the unconscious meaning of the patient's problems and behavior, be knowledgeable about how the patient's history is recapitulated in the here and now, be sensitive to how the patient copes with anxiety, and be aware of how he or she defends himself or herself from inner and outer danger. Furthermore, mental health practitioners should be able to sensitize themselves to how their patients unconsciously experience them (their transference reactions) and how, on their parts, they subjectively experience their patients, that is, how and why they have their inevitable countertransference reactions which always affect their therapeutic work with their patients.

One of the most valuable contributions of psychoanalysis to the field of mental health is to demonstrate how and why all patients resist change and to prescribe procedures to help patients overcome their resistances. Therefore, this book will not only have chapters on how psychoanalysis views behavior—adaptive and maladaptive—but it will also focus on those dimensions of psychoanalytic treatment that can be applied to all forms of psychotherapy in various types of settings—private practice, clinics, social agencies, hospitals, and elsewhere.

For well over four decades I have been applying psychoanalytic insights in my work as a clinician, supervisor, teacher, and researcher. I have found that when a particular concept is understood well, whether the concept pertains to personality theory, psychopathology, treatment, or research, much of the mystery of psychoanalysis abates and much of the hostility toward its adherents diminishes.

This book is *not* written for the practitioner who wants to practice psychoanalytic treatment. Rather, it is an attempt to provide the essentials of psychoanalytic theory and practice to those psychotherapists who can enhance their diagnostic and therapeutic armamentaria by incorporating the essentials of psychoanalysis into their daily therapeutic work with different patients in different settings. Therefore, this book is written for clinical social workers, clinical psychologists, and dynamically oriented psychiatrists working in clinics, agencies, hospitals, and private practice. It is also written for those mental health practitioners who are considering a career in psychoanalysis and want a clear introductory summary of its basic postulates.

Chapter 1 will concern itself with the dynamics of the human personality as conceived by Sigmund Freud. Here we will define and describe such concepts as the id, ego, superego, and defenses (the structural point of view); the conscious, preconscious, and unconscious states of mind (the topographic view); how each individual's past shapes his or her current functioning (the genetic point of view); instincts such as libidinal and aggressive drives and their vicissitudes (the dynamic point of view); how the individual deals with energy (the economic point of view), and, finally, we will discuss how Freudian psychoanalysis views interpersonal relationships, culture, and values.

Inasmuch as there have been many contributors to psychoanalytic theory and treatment other than Freud, Chapter 2 will deal with the major contributions of some of Freud's contemporaries such as Adler, Jung, and Rank, and some of the more recent contributions such as those from self psychology and object relations theory.

Chapter 3 will be a comprehensive discussion of how psychoanalysis explains maladaptive behavior. Here we will deal with the neuroses, psychoses, character disorders, psychosomatic illness, and other signs of pathology.

In all of the chapters in this text, we will present clinical examples to show how various concepts apply. For example, clinical illustrations will be presented to help the reader better understand the dynamics and etiology of obsessive-compulsive neuroses, paranoid schizophrenia, or the migraine headache. We will also present examples from real people of the id, ego, superego, and defenses at work, as well as other examples of how human beings express their unconscious fantasies, histories, and other dimensions of their personalities.

Chapter 4 will be a discussion of the psychoanalytic theory of therapeutic intervention. Here we will have extensive consideration of free association, dreams, transference, resistance, countertransference, and counterresistance. We will also discuss in this chapter some of the major contributions of psychoanalysis to therapeutic techniques such as confrontation, clarification, interpretation, and working through. Clinical illustrations will be given to show how psychoanalysis can help the practitioner deal with problems such as the patient who habitually comes late for interviews, refuses to pay fees, will not talk, and so on.

In the last chapter, Chapter 5, we will look at some of the research that psychoanalysis has provided for the clinician. In addition, we will discuss how a psychoanalytic orientation can be helpful to all scholars engaged in research on human functioning and psychotherapy.

I would like to thank Natalie Gilman, Chief Editor of Brunner/Mazel for encouraging me to participate in this project and for her expert editorial assistance. I would also like to express my abiding gratitude to my wife, Marcia, for typing this entire text. In addition, her excellent editorial suggestions have been very helpful. Finally, I would like to thank my patients, students, and colleagues who constantly stimulate me to learn more and more and to gain better mastery over the essentials of psychoanalysis.

ESSENTIALS OF
PSYCHOANALYSIS

1

FREUD AND HIS THEORY OF PERSONALITY

Just as psychoanalysis as a personality theory, treatment method, and research perspective has been steeped in controversy ever since its inception, Sigmund Freud, the founder of the art and science, may be regarded as one of the most controversial figures of the 20th century. Highly esteemed for his monumental discoveries, he is severely derogated for his alleged prejudices. Some aver that he is more influential than any other human being in civilization in acquainting us with the child in ourselves, while others blame him as a prime source of modern sexual libertinism and for many of the other ills of contemporary life (Roazen, 1975).

Those who regard Freud as a genius compare him to Darwin, Einstein, or Galileo (Jones, 1957). They point to his many creative contributions such as the dynamics of the unconscious, infantile sexuality and psychosexual development, the interpretation of dreams, the role of fantasies, the process of free association, the crucial importance of transference in and out of the therapeutic situation, the inevitability of human resistance to change, and many more discoveries (Freeman & Strean, 1987).

Those who condemn Freud view him as a male chauvinist who was a preserver of the status quo. They contend that he exaggerated the importance of the penis, erroneously postulated a death instinct, naively assumed that children inherit acquired characteristics, and incorrectly averred that women have weaker superegos than men (Masson, 1984, 1990).

Even among psychoanalysts and other mental health professionals there is only limited consensus on Freud's findings. During the last two decades classical Freudians have been severely criticized by object-relations experts and proponents of self psychology, to name just two dissenting groups of psychoanalysts who fault Freud for many of his positions on personality formation and treatment. Yet, there are other clinicians who claim nothing much has been discovered about personality theory or treatment since Freud entered on the psychotherapeutic stage (Malcolm, 1981).

In *A History of Psychoanalysis,* Reuben Fine (1979) points out that Freud knew little about the oral stage of development, particularly the infant's hostility toward the mother, maternal rejection, the ego and its autonomous functions, narcissism, and psychosis. Some therapists believe Freud overemphasized the importance of sexuality in the development of neuroses, while others maintain he ascribed too much to the role of aggression (Sulloway, 1979). A number of therapists suggest that Freud was too subjective as a psychoanalyst, became at times too emotionally involved with patients, while others accuse him of lacking empathy. Therapists of many persuasions regard Freud's perspective as too deterministic and his philosophy as too gloomy (Corsini, 1973).

As one reads the many biographies on Sigmund Freud (Clark, 1980; Freeman & Strean, 1987; Gay, 1988; Jones, 1957; Masson, 1985; Roazen, 1975; Sulloway, 1979), he or she learns that few remain neutral about Freud. He was and is adored and abhorred, acclaimed and disdained. Although Freud died over 50 years ago, biographies on him continue to flourish. His theories also continue to be evaluated and re-evaluated (Fine, 1962, 1979). Even his favorite jokes have been the subject of a book (Oring, 1984). Masson's (1985) publication of Freud's letters to Wilhelm Fliess, a physician who was both a collaborator and father confessor of Freud's, was a bestseller. There are currently many individuals who call themselves Freudian scholars, Freudian philosophers, Freudians, neo-Freudians, and anti-Freudians (Wollheim, 1977).

What about Sigmund Freud, the person? He was born on May 6, 1856, in Freiberg, a small town in Moravia, where his father was a businessman. For financial reasons, when Sigmund was 4 years old, his family moved to Vienna where he lived and practiced until 1938 when Austria was occupied by Hitler (Wyss, 1973).

Freud wrote little about his personal life, reluctant to have it made public. He also contended that biographers have a propensity to distort their subject. Nonetheless, a lot is known about Freud. He did say he inherited his passionate nature and temperament from his mother and his sense of humor, shrewd skepticism, liberalism, and free thinking from his father. Freud described his father as possessing a gentle disposition, loved by his children, and an optimist who was always hopefully expecting something to turn up, which unfortunately for the family finances, rarely did. Freud said he was the duplicate of his father physically and to some extent mentally. His father would often take him for walks in the dense forests of the foothills of the Carpathian Mountains half a mile from Freiberg, as Freud would later take his own children for walks in the Austrian Alps. From Jakob, Freud absorbed a love of trees, plants, and flowers (Clark, 1980; Freeman

& Strean, 1987; Gay, 1988; Jones, 1957). After the death of
his father, when Freud was 40, he wrote Fliess that he
valued his father highly and understood him very well.
He also said that nothing upsets a man more than the
death of his father (Masson, 1985).

But it was Freud's mother who played the dominant role
in his early life. As Freud was later to say, the mother is
a child's original love, and all future loves are modeled
after this first love experience. He acquired from his
mother, Amalie, a lasting sense of self-confidence that
enabled him to make discoveries that disturbed the sleep
of the world. He felt that he was a valued human being
without having to be told so. His self-esteem allowed him
to endure the most vituperative criticisms of his theories
when they were introduced to the skeptical medical profession of Vienna (Jones, 1957).

Though Freud was his mother's indisputable favorite,
he had to contend with newcomers almost continually
during the first 10 years of life. The arrival of these infants
aroused intense jealousy in him. Sigmund was followed
by a brother, Julius, who died at 8 months when Freud was
19 months old. Anna was born when Freud was 2½. Then
came Rosa, Marie (Mitzi), Pauline (Paula), Adolfine (Dolfi),
and Alexander, 10 years younger than Freud (Clark, 1980;
Jones, 1957).

It has been suggested that because Freud had so much
hostility toward his mother for having so many children, the role of the mother in the development of the
child was neglected by him (Stolorow & Atwood, 1979)
and left to a later generation of psychoanalysts to explain. In his famous case of Little Hans, a 5-year-old-boy
who suffered from a horse phobia, Freud excluded the
mother from the treatment plan. Only Freud, Hans, and
Hans's father participated in the first child guidance
case in history (Strean, 1970).

Freud always excelled as a student and scholar. He left the Gymnasium in Vienna where he had been "top boy" for 7 years and passed his University Entrance at the age of 17. Practical research and subjects ranging from archeology to literature and philosophy were all attractive to him. Although he decided to study medicine, he found limited satisfaction in the field until Ernst Bruke took him on as an assistant in the Physiological Laboratory where Freud became fascinated with physiological problems. He worked in this institute from 1876 to 1882 but was obliged to give up the idea of a career in physiological research because his financial situation would not permit it. After leaving the institute he became an assistant in the General Hospital to prepare for the practice of medicine but he continued his interest in physiological and histological investigations into the central nervous system in human beings. As a young physician he published a large number of neuropathological works on the course of the fibrous tissue in the medulla oblongata and the spinal cord (Jones, 1957; Wyss, 1973).

By 1885 Freud was appointed a lecturer in neuropathology. While studying neuropathology he became interested in nervous disorders, later called anxiety hysteria and conversion hysteria. Influenced by Charcot, one of the leading neurologists and neuropathologists of Europe, Freud concerned himself with hypnosis as a therapeutic instrument in the treatment of hysteria. Freud was able to demonstrate how some paralyses and other disorders could be overcome through hypnosis. Collaborating later with Breuer, he demonstrated that abreaction and catharsis could cure hysteria. However, when he reported his observations to his colleagues of the Viennese medical fraternity, they held him up to ridicule and did not take him seriously (Jones, 1957).

Freud's persistence and intensity never wavered and despite much opposition he refused to budge from his positions. Whether it was his notions on hypnosis, the unconscious, sexuality, aggression, free association, transference, or dreams, all notions essentially rejected by most of his colleagues, he felt strong in his aloneness and contended that his findings were based on the scientific objectivity to which he had disciplined himself. The hard struggle for existence that Freud was required to wage and endure perhaps accounted for some of his authoritarianism. He was not very tolerant of dissenters such as Adler, Jung, and Rank (Clark, 1980) and he acknowledged to his mentor Fliess that he always needed a hated enemy and an intimate friend (Masson, 1985), suggesting perhaps that he had not resolved his ambivalence toward his father.

According to Jones (1957) Freud confessed to him that he was not really a man of science, not an observer, nor an experimenter, and not a thinker. He felt that by temperament he was "a conquistador"—an adventurer with the curiosity, boldness, and tenacity that belongs to that type of being.

Freud's intensity and passionate interest are qualities that all of his biographers (Clark, 1980; Gay, 1988; Jones, 1957) note. His intense love for his mother and ambivalence toward his father helped him to discover the Oedipus complex. This intensity is also noted in his lifelong devotion to his wife Martha Bernays and his 6 children, one of whom, Anna, followed in her father's footsteps.

From his self-analysis Freud found in his own personality those conflicts, contradictions, and irrationalities he had observed in his patients, and this experience helped him gain more conviction about the essential correctness of his views. Freud was reluctant to accept the validity of any hypothesis until he had tested it out on himself. He continued his self-analysis throughout his life, reserving the last half hour of each day for this activity (Jones, 1957).

FREUD'S MAJOR CONCEPTS ON
PERSONALITY FORMATION

No conceptualization of the human personality is as complex nor as comprehensive as Freud's. Basic to understanding it is the notion of *psychic determinism* (Freud, 1939). This principle holds that in mental functioning nothing happens by chance. Everything a person feels, thinks, fantasizes, dreams, and does has a psychological motive. How individuals earn a living, whom they choose to love and marry, whom they hate, the quality and quantity of their attachments are all motivated by inner *unconscious* forces (Freud, 1905).

Although external factors are always impinging on the human being, the notions of psychic determinism and the unconscious help the mental health professional appreciate that the behaviors of individuals, couples, families, groups, institutions, and societies are not only reactions to situational variables but are also influenced and shaped by instinctual wishes, ego functions such as defenses and superego admonitions, and other idiosyncratic, internal forces. For example, two individuals working in the same plant are both fired the same day. One of them can become anxious, depressed, and suicidal while the other can feel relieved, pleased, and welcome a respite from working. The reasons for these two different responses are complex and are influenced in part by the individual's history, fantasy and dream life, self-image, and other ego functions, superego mandates, transferences toward bosses and peers, and a host of other internal factors.

A psychoanalytic perspective with its emphasis on determinism and the unconscious can help the clinician gain a better understanding of the patient's presenting problems. For example, when a prospective patient complains about a rejecting spouse or a disturbed son or daughter, a psychoanalytic perspective suggests that the complainer is deriving unconscious protection and gratification from his or her complaints. The fault-finding serves unconscious purposes.

When the mental health professional recognizes that patients are not saints or sinners, neither complete victims nor vicious perpetrators, but are vulnerable and imperfect human beings trying to discharge instinctual wishes, erect defenses against anxiety, and obey superego commands— and all almost completely unconsciously—they become less judgmental, less punitive, and more objective, trying less to impose solutions on patients, but more to understand how and why the patient has written a good part of this psychological script. Thus, when the clinician meets a husband who constantly complains his wife is sexually unresponsive, the clinician may infer that the husband unconsciously wants her to be that way. Similarly, a parent's constant complaining about a son's or daughter's belligerent behavior may reflect the parent's unconscious wish to have the child behave belligerently.

> A minister, Reverend Arnold, came to a child guidance clinic and discussed his profound shame and guilt about his son stealing automobiles. In his sixth session with a social worker, Reverend Arnold was obviously deriving much pleasure and excitement about his son's escapades as he described them in detail with a glow on his face.

> In conjoint marital treatment when Mr. Brown complained that his wife never wanted to have sex, the clinician turned to Mrs. Brown and asked about it. She confessed that she had been somewhat reluctant to have sex, but she would that night. On hearing this, Mr. Brown said anxiously, "We can wait."

> Calling a mental health clinic for an intake interview, Mr. Cole, a depressed, suicidal man who had delusions that his wife was having a

series of extramarital affairs, made an interesting slip over the phone saying, "I'm desperately in need of trouble."

Freud viewed the human personality from five distinct but intermeshing points of view: the structural, topographic, genetic, dynamic, and economic. These points of view, when combined, are called the *metapsychological approach* (Freud, 1938).

THE STRUCTURAL POINT OF VIEW

According To Freud (1923), the human mind is composed of *id*, *ego*, and *superego*. The most primitive part of the mind is the id, which is totally unconscious. The id is the repository of the drives (sex and aggression) and is concerned with their gratification. The ego, although having capacities at birth, generally develops out of experience and is the executive of the personality, mediating between the inner world of id drives, superego commands, and the demands of the external world. Some of the functions of the ego are judgment, reality testing, frustration tolerance, impulse control, and interpersonal relationships (frequently called "object relations"). The ego also erects defenses against anxiety, such as repression, denial, and reaction formation. Anxiety is the human being's way of reacting to danger either from the environment, such as news of an impending tornado, or from within, such as "news" that a forbidden impulse might emerge. By assessing a patient's ego strengths and weaknesses, the therapist can determine how well the patient is adapting because the more severe the person's disturbance, the less operative are the ego functions.

The superego may be viewed as a judge or censor of the mind, and is essentially the product of interpersonal experiences. It is divided into two parts, the conscience and the ego ideal (Freud, 1938). The conscience is that part of the superego that forbids and admonishes "thou shalt not!," while the ego ideal is the storehouse of values, ethical imperatives, and morals. It commands the person in the form of "thou shalt." When we do not follow the admonitions of the superego, we feel guilt. Guilt is superego punishment. Very often people do not know why they feel guilty inasmuch as they are punishing themselves for unconscious id wishes.

> A patient, Mrs. David, felt guilty and nauseous almost every time she had sex with her husband. It took Mrs. David and her therapist many sessions to figure out that unconsciously she made her husband an older brother. Having sex with her husband was equivalent, *in her mind*, to having forbidden incest which had to be punished.
>
> A salesman, Mr. Efros, went into a deep depression every time he made a successful sale. Exploration revealed that making a sale gratified a fantasy of "making a killing" and for that he had to be punished.

The human personality with its id, ego, and superego, can be compared to a car. The id is the engine, the ego is the driver, and the superego is the backseat driver. Just as the various parts of a car do not function in isolation, the id, ego, and superego work interdependently. Clinicians sometimes overlook the fact that a patient with a harsh superego usually has strong id wishes that cause him or her a great deal of anxiety.

> When Florence, an 18-year-old woman, told her therapist that she never wanted to have anything to do with men or sex, the therapist felt that the young lady's constant devaluation of sex and

men made her appear as if she was "protesting too much." Further sessions brought out fantasies in Florence of wanting to have "polymorphous perverse" sex—which terrified her. Her strong and punitive superego was used as a defense to stop her from feeling her strong, sexual desires.

The id, ego, and superego are always interdependently at work in every human being at all times. An example of the cooperative activity of id, ego, and superego can be seen in waking up in the morning (Strean, 1979). When the alarm goes off, many of us would like to continue to sleep (id wish). However, the superego admonishes, "You must go to work. You are committing a reprehensible act when you do not go to work!" How the demands of the id and the commands of the superego get reconciled is up to the mediating, judging ego. The ego can renounce the wish to sleep (repression) and yield to the superego's command; we will then use our ego functions—frustration tolerance, impulse control, reality testing—and mobilize ourselves to go to work. Or the ego may decide to gratify the id wish to sleep, fight the superego's commands, and go back to sleep. Yet, if we decide to sleep, the superego is still at work and to appease it we may dream we are busily at work doing our job well, or have a nightmare wherein the boss comes to our house with a gun and says, "You die if you sleep!" Whether we go to work resentfully or go back to sleep but feel guilty about it, the component parts of the psychic structure are always at work.

All mental health professionals are aided in their diagnostic and therapeutic work when they understand how the patient's id, ego, and superego are interdependently working. For example, patients who fail in work and/or love often have strong id wishes for which they are punishing themselves. These id wishes need to be discussed during therapy with a nonpunitive helper (benign superego) so that patients can see how and why they are arranging to fail.

Some of Freud's followers such as Erikson (1950), Anna Freud (1965), and Hartmann (1958) began to conceptualize the ego not only as a mediator, but also as a psychic structure that has autonomy and power of its own. They were able to demonstrate that the ego's power does not develop solely from interactions or by endowment but arises in many ways from the development of "secondary processes" (Hartmann, 1958) such as locomotion, cognition, memory, perception, and rational thought and action.

The Ego and Defenses

One of the most important ego functions to which Freud gave much attention is how the patient defends against anxiety. When an id impulse such as a sexual wish or an aggressive desire is stimulated, and the individual feels that further acknowledgment of the impulse will conflict with superego commands, the person feels anxiety. Defenses are erected to avoid experiencing anxiety. Anxiety serves as a signal of the impending danger and offers opposition to the emergence of unacceptable id wishes. Such opposition is referred to as defense, or as the defensive operation of the ego (Brenner, 1955).

Anna Freud (1946) in her popular book *The Ego and the Mechanism of Defense*, in which she elaborated on the dynamics of defenses much more than Sigmund Freud did, pointed out that in all defense mechanisms there is always an attempt to repudiate an impulse. To the id's "yes," the ego defends itself and says "no" to avoid the danger of the forbidden impulse coming into consciousness. The ego can and does use as a defense anything available to it that will lessen the danger arising from the demands of an unwanted instinctual drive.

Fine (1973) emphasized that an isolated conflict between one particular drive and an opposing anxiety rarely occurs. Rather, there are complex interactions among many drives and anxieties. A defensive struggle is rarely brought to a successful conclusion by one particular activity. Defenses may be more or less successful; they may work under certain circumstances or be insufficient under others.

Seemingly irrational, provocative behavior that appears disruptive to interpersonal relationships can often be understood and related to with empathy by clinicians if they remain fully aware of the fact that all human beings defend themselves from ideas, thoughts, and feelings that arouse anxiety. In *The Ego and Mechanisms of Defense*, Anna Freud (1946) describes a number of defense mechanisms that are used by most of us when danger presents itself and anxiety is experienced. It should be mentioned that the kinds of danger that arouse anxiety are several: loss of the love object, that is, the loved person; loss of love from an important person; castration; and superego disapproval—and their attendant unpleasant affects (Freud, 1896). The following are some of the defense mechanisms universally utilized to cope with anxiety.

1. *Repression*—An attempt to exclude from awareness feelings and thoughts that evoke anxiety. In repression, the feelings and thoughts may have been experienced consciously at one time, or the repressive work may have stopped ideas and feelings from ever reaching consciousness. For example, an individual may have consciously experienced hateful feelings toward a parent or sibling but, because of the anxiety evoked, blocked the feelings from awareness. Or an individual, in order to protect himself or herself from

feeling the unpleasantness and dread of anxiety, never allows any hostile thoughts or feelings to reach consciousness.

2. *Displacement*—Feelings and thoughts directed toward one person or object are directed toward another person. For example, a boy who finds himself feeling anxious about sexual feelings toward his mother falls in love with an actress. Or, voyeuristic fantasies that involve an interest and curiousity in the genitals are directed toward a less anxiety-provoking subject such as bacteriology.

3. *Reaction formation*—A painful idea or feeling is replaced by its opposite. A young girl, for example, who cannot tolerate hateful feelings toward her newly arrived brother keeps saying, "I love my new brother!"

4. *Projection*—An intolerable idea or feeling is ascribed to someone else. For example, it can be hypothesized that because the late Senator Joseph McCarthy could not tolerate his own homosexual wishes, he spent much time compiling lists of men in the State Department who, according to McCarthy, were hiding their homosexuality.

5. *Isolation*—Painful ideas are separated from feelings associated with them. To face the full impact of sexual or aggressive thoughts and feelings, the ideas and affects are kept apart, For example, the thought of shouting obscenities in a church is kept separate from all the rage about being in church. Thus, in isolation the individual may have fleeting thoughts of an aggressive or sexual nature without any emotional accompaniment.

6. *Undoing*—Trying to remove an offensive act, either by pretending it was not done or by atoning for it. For example, a boss hates an employee and wishes to fire him. Instead he "counsels him out" and gives him gifts for years, thereby diminishing in his mind what he thinks he has done.

7. *Regression*—A retreat to an earlier form of behavior and psychic organization because of anxiety in the present. For example, under the impact of anxiety stirred up by wishes to masturbate, a teenager returns to an earlier form of behavior and resumes sucking his thumb.

8. *Introjection*—The opposite of projection; the individual "takes inside" him or herself what is threatening. For example, a youngster feels strong anxiety about losing a parent's love when the latter admonishes her for not cleaning her room. To cope with the anxiety, she tells herself constantly, "You are a bad girl" and slaps herself from time to time.

9. *Denial*—Pretending that a threatening situation is not there because the situation is distressing to cope with. A child comes home and no one is there. He says to himself, "They are here. I'll find them soon."

10. *Identification with the aggressor*—Doing unto someone else what aroused anxiety when it was done to oneself. A child is subjected to a tonsillectomy. He or she then puts on a toy stethoscope and goes around taking out the tonsils of peers.

Defenses may also function constructively, making thought and action more efficient. These are referred to as adaptive mechanisms or autonomous ego functions (Moore & Fine, 1990). For example, in reaction formation a youngster's preoccupation with cleanliness that wards off wishes to soil may serve him or her in good stead with parents, teachers, and others. It may also build self-esteem and body image.

THE TOPOGRAPHIC POINT OF VIEW

In his 1915 paper entitled "The Unconscious," Freud (1915a) proposed the topographic point of view. This perspective refers to the *conscious, preconscious,* and *unconscious* states of mind. The conscious is that part of our mental life of which we are fully aware at any time; for example, the time we know we feel sexual excitement. The preconscious refers to thoughts and feelings that can be brought into consciousness fairly easily; for example, with some external stimulation we can feel sexual excitement. The unconscious refers to thoughts, feelings, and desires of which we are not aware but which very much influence our behavior.

The unconscious is the depository of sexual and aggressive drives, defenses, superego mandates, memories, and feelings that have been repressed. It is only when unconscious wishes, defenses, or superego mandates are discharged in dreams, fantasies, or neurotic symptoms that the unconscious becomes known. Otherwise the unconscious acts silently and completely beyond awareness.

The *system unconscious*, as Freud (1915a) referred to it, is characterized by primary process thinking, and the preconscious and conscious systems by secondary process thinking which employs logic and reason. Freud postulated a censorship barrier between the unconscious and preconscious and between the preconscious and conscious. The *primary process* is best observed in dreams that are frequently illogical and unrealistic, for example, walking on air. One of the devices of the primary process is *condensation*—one idea standing for many, much as symbols do in works of art. Another device is *displacement*—the shifting of ideas to a different area so that in a dream or fantasy one may revile a deceased parent while really being angry at a spouse. A third device of the primary process is *symbolization*, whereby unconscious meanings are concealed by what is represented; for example, a patient disguises her wish to hug her therapist by dreaming that she hugs the conductor of a subway car. In contrast to the primary process, the *secondary process*, which governs conscious thinking, is characterized by rationality and logic.

One of the basic tenets of psychoanalysis is that the unconscious is always operative in all behavior, adaptive and maladaptive. This perspective leads the clinician to ask how and why a particular patient aids and abets the very problem he or she brings to therapy.

> In marital therapy, Mrs. Grover always berated her husband for his chronic alcoholism. Although Mr. Grover was defensive each time his wife was critical of him, he was concomitantly trying to stop drinking. When Mr. Grover was abstinent for 3 weeks, Mrs. Grover thought it would be a good idea to celebrate her husband's accomplishment. Therefore, she went out and bought him a present—a bottle of Scotch. It took her a long time to realize that she had a strong unconscious investment in maintaining her husband's alcoholism.

The psychoanalytically oriented practitioner always wants to know the unconscious purpose of painful symptomotology. He or she wants to know what unconscious protection, gratification, or punishment a migraine headache, sexual impotence, marital conflict, or parent-child disharmony serves.

One of the major objectives of psychoanalytic therapy is to make the unconscious conscious. The manner in which this is done is starting from the surface, that is, working with the patient's conscious ideas and feelings first, then moving on to discuss preconscious ideas and then unconscious feelings, thoughts, and memories.

> Paula Hirsch came for therapy because at the age of 40 she had very little sexual satisfaction with men. As she discussed her conscious fears with her therapist, Paula slowly learned that

behind her fears were strong preconscious wishes to dominate men sadistically. As this "wish-fear" was explored in breadth and depth, Paula slowly discovered that she had strong incestuous fantasies, which were very much repressed, toward her father and brother.

THE GENETIC POINT OF VIEW

Each individual's historical past participates in and shapes his or her present functioning. Psychoanalytic theory postulates that all individuals experience the present based in many ways on their subjective past. Particularly in our interpersonal relationships, we tend to ascribe to contemporaries qualities that really belong to those in our past, such as parents and siblings (Fenichel, 1945; Freud, 1905; Fine, 1982).

During the first 5 or 6 years of life the child experiences a series of dynamically differentiated stages that are of enormous importance for the formation of personality. In the oral stage (from birth to about age 18 months) the mouth is the principal focus of dynamic activity; in the anal phase (from about 18 months to 3 years) the child turns his or her interests to elimination functions; in the phallic stage (ages 3 to 6) he or she forms the rudiments of gender identity; in latency (ages 7 to 11) erotic interests are quiescent; and at puberty there is a reemergence of biological drives, particularly of oedipal interests that emerged during the phallic phase. Ambivalence toward parents is also characteristic of puberty and adolescence (Fine, 1973; Freud, 1905).

According to Freudian theory, children are *polymorphous perverse*; that is, they can derive pleasure from any bodily activity. From the ages of 3 to 5 the child engages in extensive sexual exploration and tries to find out how babies are conceived. Frequently children think that babies are conceived by eating and are born through the rectum; often they view sexual intercourse as an act of sadism. Freud was the first to demonstrate clearly that sex is never a subject of indifference for any child in any family or culture (Fine, 1962). A central concept in Freudian theory is the Oedipus complex, which occurs during the ages of 3 to 6. In most societies the familial arrangements are such that they create in the child a wish to replace the parent of the same sex and have sexual contact with the parent of the opposite sex. Children expect to be punished for their incestuous wishes and rivalry, and as they learn to monitor their oedipal wishes, the superego develops. Freud suggested that the "superego is the heir to the Oedipus complex" (Freud, 1923).

Inasmuch as all children have omnipotent fantasies, boys envy girls and girls envy boys. Boys often suffer from breast and vagina envy and girls suffer from penis envy. Freud (1905, 1923) was able to demonstrate that in all human organisms "the grass always appears to be greener on the other side."

Central to the genetic point of view are two important concepts, *regression* and *fixation*. As we discussed in the section on defenses, regression implies that the individual has successfully mastered certain psychosocial tasks but returns to previous less mature modes of psychosocial functioning. For example, an adult who has guilt and anxiety about his or her sexual wishes may cope with the discomfort by getting drunk frequently (from genital back to anal level). Regression implies that the individual has successfully mastered certain psychosocial tasks but he or she returns to previous, less mature gratifications when certain demands in the present induce anxiety.

The term fixation is used to describe individuals who have never matured beyond a certain point of psychosocial development and are unable, in many ways, to mature further. It is not always easy to determine whether a particular symptom or interpersonal difficulty is a regression or fixation. The same symptom may be either.

> Mr. Isaacs and Mr. Joseph were both seen at a mental health center for alcoholism. As Mr. Isaac's history and other dimensions of his personality were assessed, it was clear that his alcoholism was a regression. He had married a woman whom he made into a mother and became sexually impotent with her. To get away from his wife, he would go out with the boys. However, closeness with "the boys" activated anxiety for him since he could not accept his homosexual fantasies toward "the boys." To rid himself of this anxiety, he drank.
>
> Mr. Joseph's mother died at his birth and he was reared in a series of foster homes, never having a stable mother figure. Inasmuch as he could not trust anybody to provide him with gratification, he turned to his bottle for pleasure. He was fixated at the oral level and had not matured beyond it.

The determination of where the patient's struggle is— that is, at what level of maturational development is the patient?—has extremely important implications for treatment. If the patient is fixated at an oral level of development, he will probably need a therapeutic experience that will enable him to express his oral aggression and mistrust of maternal figures, including the therapist, so that he can then move up the psychosexual ladder with the therapist serving as maturational agent (Strean, 1979). However, if he regresses to orality because he has sexual conflicts, the sexual conflicts are what need attention in treatment.

THE DYNAMIC POINT OF VIEW

The dynamic point of view refers to Freud's instinct theory, which is concerned with the libidinal and aggressive drives (Freud, 1915a). Nature and nurture are two variables that are always present in the development of the human being, the drives or instincts representing the "nature" factor.

An instinct has four characteristics: a source, an aim, an object, and an impetus. The source is a bodily condition such as hunger or sexual tension. The aim is to release tension and receive pleasure. The object includes both the object on which the drive is focused, for example, food, and all the activities necessary to secure it, such as going to the refrigerator, ingesting, and chewing. The impetus of an instinct is its strength, which is determined by the force or intensity of the underlying bodily state, for example, hunger, sexual tension, aggressive wish.

THE ECONOMIC POINT OF VIEW

The economic point of view stresses the quantitative factor in mental functioning. According to this principle, all behavior is regulated by the desire to dispose of psychological energy. Energy is discharged by forming *cathexes*, that is, something or somebody is *cathected* if it is emotionally significant to a person.

The energy concept is among the most controversial in psychoanalysis and many theoreticians and clinicians contend that it can be dispensed with entirely (Fine, 1973).

Although the metapsychological approach, which involves the dynamic, genetic, topographic, structural, and economic points of view, comprises the major dimensions necessary for a complete psychoanalytic understanding of the human personality, Freud and other psychoanalysts have elaborated on the metapsychological approach by offering further notions on interpersonal relationships, culture, and values.

INTERPERSONAL INTERACTIONS, CULTURE, AND VALUES

Interpersonal Interactions

According to psychoanalytic theory, how an individual relates interpersonally is essentially based on how he or she experienced himself or herself vis-à-vis parents, siblings, and other family memers. As children interact with family members they introject their experiences and give them meaning. For example, a child might learn that if he or she works hard and complies with all of his or her parents' mandates, he or she will be loved, but should the child not adhere to parental dictates, he or she might be unloved and abandoned. If this is the message the child incorporates, it will be brought into most of his or her interpersonal relationships. As a wife, for example, this person will become very anxious if she disagrees with her husband and at work will be frightened unless she submits to the boss.

The vicissitudes of interpersonal relationships depend very heavily on *transferences* from the individual's family. Despite the fact that the concept of transference is used chiefly in psychotherapy, it is a universal characteristic of human beings (Freud, 1912). The kinds of experiences that offered us gratification in our families we tend to pursue; those that frustrated us and induced pain tend to be avoided.

> Sally Katz, a woman in her 30s, experienced her mother as an engulfing person who imposed "too much of herself" on Sally. Whenever Sally was in a close relationship, particularly a love relationship with a man, she worried that she would lose all of her autonomy; consequently, she fled the relationship. In her therapy, she experienced her female therapist the same way. As she saw how much she had to repeat her relationship with her mother with others, eventually she could acknowledge a hidden wish in herself to turn the world into a symbiotic mother.

Freud (1914b) pointed out that children proceed from a narcissistic stage in which they are concerned essentially with themselves, to an anaclitic stage, in which they are dependent on someone else, and eventually to a stage of object love. In object love there is a mutuality between one person and another, and this love involves a synthesis of tender and erotic feelings toward the opposite sex. Other writers, such as Hartmann (1964), to whom we will refer in Chapter 3, have added to Freud's notions on interpersonal relationships. Hartmann proposed a movement in relationships from "need-gratifying" ones to those where there is mutuality and "constancy." Fine (1975) suggested that relationships start off as "attachment" in infancy and move to "admiration" (of the parents), then to "intimacy," and finally to "devotion." All love relationships, according to Fine, have these components.

Culture

In *Totem and Taboo* (1913b), Freud demonstrated that the same psychological mechanisms are found in all cultures. Although the same libidinal and aggressive drives exist in all human beings and societies, they are molded in different ways by different societies.

One of the major attempts to unify psychoanalysis and the study of culture was made by Kardiner (1939, 1945). He contributed the term "basic personality structure" to designate a group of character traits in the modal individual of a particular culture. Examples of American character traits are "ambitiousness" and "greed."

Neuroses and psychoses are relative to a particular culture. Every culture has its own neurosis, its own superego or ethos, "a set of goals and ideals that are held out as desirable to young and old" (Fine, 1990, p. 103).

Values

The question of whether there are any values inherent in psychoanalysis has been much debated. Freud did not speak much of values but did take the position that the mature person is one who can love and work with pleasure. Fine (1982) attempted to extend Freud's image of love and work and has argued that psychotherapy is the first scientific attempt to make people happy. His "analytic ideal" involves pursuing pleasure, releasing positive emotions, eliminating hatred and other negative emotions, acquiring a meaningful role in the family and sense of identity in the larger society, engaging in some satisfying form of work, pursuing some form of creative activity, and being able to communicate with other people.

In his more recent work, *Love and Work: The Value System of Psychoanalysis* (1990), Fine demonstrates how psychoanalysis is, in fact, a system of positive values that is most likely to lead to emotional health and happiness.

In a paper entitled "The Current Status of Psychoanalysis," a leading authority in the field, Otto Kernberg (1993) concludes:

Psychoanalysis as a theory of psychic functioning contains an unparalleled explanatory power for
psychopathology in general and for linking the
biological, psychological, social, and cultural de-
terminants of human behavior in particular. Psychoanalysis increases an understanding, for example, of the early development of the human
infant, affect theory and the neuropsychology of
memory at its boundary with biological sciences;
an understanding of love relations, marital conflict, group regression, and organizational morale
at its boundary with social sciences; an understanding of mythology, mass psychology, ideology,
and aesthetics at its boundary with the cultural
milieu. (p. 47)

RECOMMENDED READINGS *

For more details on Freud's life, see *The Life and Work of
Sigmund Freud*, written by Jones, a loyal follower of
Freud's. Less idealizing and more historically valid are
books by historians: Clark, *Freud: The Man and the Cause*;
and Gay who wrote *Freud: A Life for Our Time*.

For a stimulating discussion on how Freud's life story
contributed to his psychoanalytic notions, see Stolorow
and Atwood's *Faces in a Cloud: Subjectivity in Personality
Theory*. Freud's relationships with his colleagues is well
discussed in Roazen's *Freud and His Followers*. Freud's
letters to his colleague and mentor Fleiss may be found in
Masson's *The Complete Letters of Sigmund Freud to
Wilhelm Fliess, (1887–1904)*.

His relationships with women are examined in
Appignanesi and Forrester's *Freud's Women* and also in
Freeman and Strean's *Freud and Women*.

*Dates of publications, place, and publisher will be found in the reference list.

For a fuller explication of Freud's metapsychological approach see Brenner's *An Elementary Textbook of Psychoanalysis*. Also, Fine's *Freud: A Critical Re-evaluation of His Theories* is a sophisticated assessment of Freud's personality theories as well as his views on psychopathology and treatment.

For social workers interested in applying psychoanalytic theory to social work practice see Strean's *Psychoanalytic Theory and Social Work Practice*.

A discussion on psychoanalysis's views of interpersonal relationships, culture, and values may be found in Fine's *Love and Work: The Value System of Psychoanalysis*.

For the reader who wishes to read Freud's work directly, he or she is directed to the 24 volumes of Strachey's *Standard Edition*, and for those who would like to read a critical response to Freud and psychoanalysis, see Masson's *Final Analysis: The Making and Unmaking of a Psychoanalyst* or Sulloway's *Freud: Biologist of the Mind*.

2

MODIFIERS OF FREUD'S PERSONALITY THEORY

Since the inception of psychoanalysis, many psychoanalytic scholars and clinicians have modified or added various concepts to Freud's metapsychological approach. In this chapter we will briefly review concepts and constructs of those psychoanalytic writers who have had a significant impact on psychonalysis by modifying or extending traditional Freudian personality theory.

ALFRED ADLER

A valued contemporary of Freud's, Alfred Adler eventually became estranged from his mentor, rejecting many of Freud's theories on psychosexual development and treatment. The theory of personality that Adler postulated is an extremely economical one. A few concepts explain his whole theoretical structure (Adler, 1927; Ansbacher & Ansbacher, 1956; Orgler, 1963).

ADLER'S MAJOR CONCEPTS

STRIVING FOR SUPERIORITY

There are three stages in Adler's thinking concerning the primary motive in the human being. By 1908 Adler was disagreeing with Freud on the importance of the sexual instincts and began to reach the conclusion that aggression was more of a prime mover of behavior than sexuality. The aggressive drive was introduced by Adler as a unitary instinct in which the primary drives lose their autonomy and find themselves subordinated to this one drive. The aggressive instinct is the biological source of psychic energy utilized when individuals overcome their organic inferiorities through compensation (Adler, 1927).

Later Adler renounced the importance of instincts and felt that the aggressive drive was essentially a mode of striving to adapt to life's tasks (Adler, 1941). He conceptualized this later notion as the "will to power." Adler identified power with masculinity and weakness with femininity. It was in the development of the "will to power" that Adler postulated the idea of the "masculine protest," a form of compensation that both men and women indulge in when they feel inadequate and inferior (Adler, 1927).

Eventually Adler abandoned the "will to power" in favor of the notion "striving for superiority" to which he committed himself for the rest of his life. By "superiority" Adler was not referring to social distinction or position but to "self-realization" or "self-actualization." Adler felt that the striving for superiority was innate and that it manifested itself in many different ways. The neurotic person's striving for superiority is primarily selfish and egocentric; the "normal" person strives for goals that are primarily social (Ansbacher & Ansbacher, 1956).

ORGANIC INFERIORITY

Evolving from his medical interest, Adler postulated that each individual, because of his or her constitutional predispositions, has organic deficits. He recognized that external demands and environmental conditions could induce stress in the organism, and the vulnerable organ would be the first site of maladaptation (Adler, 1927).

Adler broadened his work on organic inferiority and shifted his focus from objective work on physical organs to the study of subjective feelings of inferiority. People not only compensate for organic deficits as Demosthenes did when he became an orator to cope with his speech disorder, stuttering, but also compensate for subjective feelings of inferiority. An air of bravado can compensate for a feeling of unmanliness, and name-dropping can compensate for feelings of social or intellectual incompetence. To rationalize failure, Adler contended that individuals develop symptoms such as migraine headaches or asthma (Hall & Lindzey, 1957).

Adler asserted that the feeling of inferiority is not an abnormal or pathological phenomenon. The child feels inferior next to the adult, and all adults when they reach a certain level of competence in any pursuit always strive for a higher level of development. When the individual attains the next level of aspiration, he or she begins to feel inferior again and the upward movement is initiated once more. Although Adler believed that inferiority feelings were painful, he did not take the position that the relief of these feelings was necessarily pleasurable. Perfection, not pleasure, was for him the goal of life (Adler, 1927).

FICTIONAL FINALISM

Adler (1927) contended that human beings deceive themselves by accepting fictions that become their final goals. Fictional finalism implies that much of the individual's behavior can be explained by understanding his or her final goals.

Although the final goal may be a fiction, it is an ideal towards which human beings strive. The more people are dominated by inferiority feelings, the more their goals are unrealistic. The healthy individual sets realistic goals and faces reality when required to do so (Adler, 1927).

LIFE-STYLE

Each individual, according to Adler, has a unique way of striving for goals and reaching a superior position. Based on the individual's constitution, early life experiences, and inferiorities, he or she finds unique means to arrange his or her life. If an individual feels intellectually inferior, intellectual superiority will be his or her life goal and will organize much of his or her life in the pursuit of knowledge. Napoleon's conquering life-style could be attributed to his reaction to his inferior height and Hitler's strong yearning for world domination could be explained by his inferiority feelings as a sexual man (Ansbacher & Ansbacher, 1956).

THE CREATIVE SELF

The creative self is that part of the personality that acts upon the facts in the environment and transforms them into some coherent meaning. The creative self arranges the goals of life as well as the means towards the goals. The notion of a creative self states that the individual makes his or her personality. Although heredity endows the individual with certain abilities, environment induces important and specific impressions (Orgler, 1963).

SOCIAL INTEREST

Towards the end of his career, Adler encapsulated his humanitarian and social philosophy, which emphasized cooperation and altruism, into the concept of social interest. Adler believed that social interest is inborn and that the human being is a social creature by nature. Through education at home and school the child learns to subordinate private gain for social altruism (Adler, 1929).

ORDER OF BIRTH AND EARLIEST MEMORIES

Adler contended that the life style of individuals was very much related to their ordinal position in their families. The firstborn is usually ambitious, trying to maintain a superior position in the family. The second child tends to be rebellious and envious, and the youngest child tends to be impulsive and demanding.

Although he did not emphasize the importance of the past, early experiences, or the unconscious, Adler did assert that the individual's earliest memories were an important key to understanding his or her basic life style (Adler, 1927, 1929).

THE NEUROTIC SYMPTOM

Adler viewed the neurotic symptom as an attempt to attract the attention of other persons. This is what many clinicians imply when they refer to "secondary gain" in neurotic illness. The choice of symptoms is facilitated by organic inferiority, and the more pervasive the inferiority, the more profound is the need to attract attention and, therefore, the more severe the illness.

Alfred Adler's concepts are utilized by many mental health workers, particularly social workers who are interested in the social context of their clients, interpersonal interactions, and the unique life styles of many different groups. Adler's concepts have provided sustenance and some theoretical rationale for several of social work's values and practice principles (Strean, 1975). Many psychologists and educators also endorse a number of his concepts (Orgler, 1963).

OTTO RANK

Otto Rank came across Freud's work in 1904 when Rank was 20. He was particularly fascinated by "free association" and with Freud's notions on dreams. According to Rank's main biographer, Jessie Taft (1958), after reading Freud's writings Rank went through what could be called a religious and ecstatic revelation.

In 1905 when Rank had completed his training at a technical school and was working in a machine shop, a meeting between Freud and Rank was arranged through Alfred Adler. Freud was quite attracted to the creative young man and was particularly fascinated with Rank's book *The Artist,* published in English in 1932 and called *Art and the Artist.*

Although the collaboration with Freud was a mutually productive one, when Rank "emancipated" himself and expressed it in part in his book *The Trauma of Birth* (1924), the separation from Freud was indeed traumatic for Rank. He became more depressed and eventually alienated from Freud. Although constantly battling depressions and an ugly self-image, Rank's contributions have been many. His books *The Trauma of Birth* (1924), *Art and the Artist* (1932), and *Will Therapy, Truth and Reality* (1945) have been the most influential.

RANK'S MAJOR CONCEPTS

BIRTH TRAUMA

In *The Trauma of Birth* (1924) Rank constructed a new approach to the genesis of mental development. Based on the separation anxiety that every baby experiences when born, Rank interpreted this "primal anxiety" as the most important element for the future development of the individual and also as the source of neurosis. According to Rank, the fixation on the mother is because of the freedom from pain that she affords, the memory of which is recorded at the deepest levels of the unconscious and reproduced in analysis.

According to Rank, the whole of childhood is needed to overcome the birth trauma, and neurotics are those who do not succeed. The primal anxiety emanating from the birth trauma is transferred to almost any person or object, yet unconsciously the child is merely expressing feelings of vulnerability because he or she is no longer comforted by the mother's womb.

Rank agreed with Freud that weaning and other developmental problems induce anxiety but alleged that all later anxieties are in many ways derived from the birth trauma. Just as primal anxiety forms the basis for every subsequent fear or anxiety, primal pleasure is the basis for every other pleasure. Sucking and excretion are viewed by Rank as seeking to maintain the prenatal state, and all clinging to infantile modes is a wish to restore the original state. Infantile sexuality is interpreted as the search for the lost memory of an earlier abode and the real interest of the child is how to get back inside.

THE WILL

Rank (1945) argued that the organism is not merely a passive, helpless tool but is or can become an initiating power that selects, organizes, modifies, and recreates what it assimilates. The will is a guiding organization of the self that both utilizes creatively and controls instinctual drives.

The will serves the process of individualization. Children make their first acquaintance with the will in the form of the "counter-will." Only when children are able to say "no," to oppose the demands of grown-ups, can children grasp the notion that they have a will of their own.

NEUROSES

Rank's view of neuroses derives from his concept of will. In contrast to the "average man," both neurotics and creative individuals, that is, artists, have broken with the mandates of society. The "average man" continues to live his life within the deceptive unity of the collective social order and refuses to accept himself as an individual.

The "neurotic," although recognizing the necessity for self-realization, has broken down on the way and can neither move back to the level of the average man nor move toward creative productivity (Rank, 1924).

In psychotherapy, Rank's aim is to enable the neurotic, who is vacillating between the bonds of the average man and the individualization and freedom of the artist, to accept his own will and individuality without feeling guilty or anxious about it.

Many writers (Strean, 1975; Taft, 1958) have acknowledged that Rank is quite difficult to understand and this may be one of the reasons why his ideas have not had as great an impact as they could have had. Nonetheless, some of his notions such as separation-individuation, will and will therapy, and end-setting in treatment are part of the practice wisdom of many clinicians.

CARL JUNG

A strong personality like that possessed by Freud attracted and then repelled other strong personalities (Hall & Lindzey, 1957). This was the history of Adler's and Rank's relationships to Freud and his ideas and it is also the story of Jung. At one time considered the heir apparent to Freud, Jung became estranged from Freud and founded his own school of psychoanalysis, which became known as Analytical Psychology (Jung, 1915).

One of the distinctive features of Jung's view of the human being is that it combines teleology with causality. The human being's behavior is conditioned not only by individual and racial history (causality) but also by aims and aspirations (teleology). Jung's view of personality looks ahead to the person's future. The person "lives by aims" as well as causes. Jung's theory also places a great deal of emphasis on the racial and phylogenetic foundations of personality. He sees the individual personality as the product and container of its ancestral history. There is a racially preformed and collective personality, according to Jung, which reaches out selectively into the world of experience and is modified by the experiences it receives (Jung, 1917).

JUNG'S MAJOR CONCEPTS

The total personality or "psyche" consists of a number of interacting systems (Hall & Lindzey, 1957; Jung, 1915, 1917, 1928).

THE EGO

The conscious mind, the ego, is made up of conscious perceptions, memories, thoughts, and feelings. It is responsible for one's feeling of identity.

THE PERSONAL UNCONSCIOUS

A region adjoining the ego, the personal unconscious consists of experiences that were once repressed or too weak to make a conscious impression upon the person.

COMPLEXES

An organized group of feelings, thoughts, perceptions, and memories that exist in the personal unconscious. A complex may behave like an autonomous personality that has a mental life of its own such as "the mother complex." The mother complex is derived from "racial" experiences with mothers and the child's experiences with his or her mother.

THE COLLECTIVE UNCONSCIOUS

A storehouse of latent memory traces inherited from the past. They are predispositions that set us to react to the world in a selective fashion. What a person learns as a result of experiences is influenced by the collective unconscious, which exercises a guiding influence over the person's behavior from the beginning of life.

ARCHETYPE

A universal thought form or idea that contains a large element of emotion. This thought form creates images that correspond to some aspect of the conscious situation. For example, the archetype of the mother produces an image of a mother figure which is then identified with the actual mother. "The baby inherits a preformed conception of a generic mother which determines in part how the baby will perceive his mother. The baby's perception is also influenced by the nature of the mother and by the infant's experiences with her" (Hall & Lindzey, 1957, p. 82). Some archetypes have evolved so far as to warrant their being considered as separate systems within the psyche or personality. These are the persona, the anima and the animus, and the shadow.

THE PERSONA

This is a mask worn by the person in response to both the environment and inner archetypal needs. It is similar to a role in a social situation (Jung, 1928).

THE ANIMA AND THE ANIMUS

The feminine side of man's personality is the anima and the masculine archetype in woman is called the animus. Conditioned by biological factors, they are the products of interpersonal experiences. Living with women throughout the ages, man has become feminized; by living with man, woman has become masculinized (Hall & Lindzey, 1957; Jung, 1928).

THE SHADOW

Consisting of the animal instincts, the shadow archetype is responsible for the appearance in consciousness and in behavior of "unpleasant" and "socially reprehensible" thoughts, feelings, and actions. These may either be hidden from public view by the persona or repressed into the personal unconscious (Jung, 1928).

THE SELF

This defined as the midpoint of personality, around which all of the other systems are constellated. It holds these systems together and provides the personality with unity, equilibrium, and stability. It is a point midway between the conscious and the unconscious. The self is life's goal, a goal that is striven for but rarely reached (Jung, 1953).

THE ATTITUDES

According to Jung (1933), there are two major attitudes, *extraversion* and *introversion*. The extraverted attitude orients the person toward the external, objective world; the introverted attitude orients the person toward the inner, subjective world. These two opposing attitudes are present in everyone but one of them is dominant and conscious while the other is subordinate and unconscious.

THE FUNCTIONS

According to Jung (1933), four fundamental functions are *thinking, feeling, sensing,* and *intuiting.* Thinking is ideational and intellectual. It is the function used to comprehend the world and oneself. Feeling is the *value* of things with reference to the subject. This function gives the individual his or her subjective experiences of pleasure, pain, anger, fear, sorrow, and joy. Sensing is the perceptual or reality function. It yields concrete facts or representations of the world. Intuition is perception by way of unconscious processes. The intuitive person goes beyond facts, feelings, and ideas and constructs models of reality.

Although every individual possesses all four functions, usually one of them is more highly differentiated than the others. This is called the *superior* function. The least differentiated of the four functions is called the *inferior* function. It is repressed and unconscious.

PSYCHIC ENERGY

Opposition exists everywhere in the personality and conflict is a basic fact of life, according to Jung (1915). All of this is propelled by psychic energy. Psychic energy originates from the metabolic processes of the body. It is a hypothetical construct and therefore cannot be measured. The "amount" of psychic energy invested in an element of the personality is called the *value* of that element. When we speak of placing a high value upon a particular idea or feeling, we imply that the idea or feeling exerts a powerful force in directing behavior (Hall & Lindzey, 1957).

THE CONSTELLATING POWER OF A COMPLEX

This consists of the number of groups of items that are brought into association by the nuclear element of the complex.

Thus, if one has a strong patriotic complex it means that the nucleus, love of one's country, will produce constellations of experiences around it. One such constellation may consist of important events in the history of one's nation, while another may be a postitive feeling towards national leaders and heroes. A very patriotic person is predisposed to fit any new experience into one of the constellations associated with patriotism (Hall & Lindzey, 1957, p. 92).

Jung discovered the existence of complexes by using the word association test (Jung, 1918). This test consists of a standard list of words that are read one at a time to the person being tested. The subject is instructed to reply with the first word that enters his or her mind. Hesitation usually indicates that the word is connected with a complex.

THE PRINCIPLE OF EQUIVALENCE

This principle states that if energy is removed from one system, for example, the ego, it will appear in another system, for example, the persona. If a particular "value" weakens or disappears, the sum of energy represented by the value will not be lost from the psyche but will reappear in a new value.

THE PRINCIPLE OF ENTROPY

This principle states that the distribution of energy in the psyche seeks an equilibrium or balance. When Jung asserts that self-actualization is the goal of psychic development, he means that the personality strives to move toward an equilibrium (Jung, 1928).

STAGES OF DEVELOPMENT

The concept of development, though central to Jung's ideas, is not too concerned with childhood development.

Life, according to Jung, is divided into two periods. The first half involves establishing one's place in the world and choosing a mate, occupation, values, and interests. The second half is concerned with confronting and adapting to mortality. The sequential progression of life is directed toward *individuation*, a lifelong process in which a person becomes "a psychological individual, that is, a separate indivisibility or whole" (Jung, 1963, p. 383).

"Individuation involves a continual pressure to make available to consciousness the potential latent in the original structure and to relieve inherent tensions by reconciling or balancing opposites" (Moore & Fine, 1990, p. 18). Individuation emphasizes three things: (1) the goal of the process is the development of the whole personality; (2) individuation does not occur in a state of isolation but presupposes and includes collective relationships; and (3) individuation involves a degree of opposition to social norms (Jung, 1928).

SELF

In analytical psychology the self has distinct meanings: (1) the totality of the psyche; (2) the tendency of the psyche to function in an ordered and patterned manner; (3) the psyche's tendency to produce images and symbols of something beyond the ego, for example, God; and (4) the psychological unity of the human infant at birth (Moore & Fine, 1990).

In *Theories of Personality*, Hall and Lindzey (1957) conclude their assessment of Jung with the following tribute:

> When all is said and done, Jung's theory of personality...stands as one of the most remarkable achievements in modern thought. The originality and audacity of Jung's thinking have few parallels in recent scientific history, and no other

man aside from Freud has opened up more conceptual windows into what Jung would choose to
call "the soul of man." His ideas merit the closest
attention from every serious student of psychology. (p. 110)

KAREN HORNEY

Originally a dedicated Freudian, like Adler and Jung,
Horney broke with Freud and in the 1930s started her own
"school." Horney was interested in the cultural forces that
contribute to the etiology of psychological disorders, and
when she began to question childhood sexuality, instincts,
the Oedipus complex, penis envy, and other Freudian
notions, her ideas came into conflict with those of her
colleagues at the New York Psychoanalytic Institute. In
1941, the break came; she left the New York Institute and
founded the Association for the Advancement of Psychoanalysis, a training institute established primarily for
psychiatrists to train them in Horney's orientation to
psychoanalysis (Alexander, Eisenstein, & Grotjahn, 1965).
As is true with Jung and Adler, Horney's training institute
still flourishes.

Horney's many books have been utilized not only by
many professionals, but also by laymen, physicians, and
educators. Among her most popular books are *The Neurotic Personality of Our Time* (1937), *Feminine Psychology*
(1967), *Our Inner Conflicts* (1945), and *Neurosis and
Human Growth* (1950).

Although Horney retained Freud's notions of psychic
determinism, unconscious motivation, and repression,
she contended that much of human behavior is learned
and shaped by ongoing interactions. In her rejection of
psychosexual development, she stressed that conflicts
like penis envy and the Oedipus complex derived exclusively from familial interaction. Conflict always arises out

of social conditions, according to Horney, and it exists because of the inconsistencies in a culture which are then transmitted by parents to children. Some of the conflicts in American society that she noted were competition versus brotherly love, stimulation of wishes versus frustrations in reality, autonomy and freedom versus arbitrary limitations (Horney, 1937, 1950).

HORNEY'S MAJOR CONCEPTS

BASIC ANXIETY

Horney's organizing concept is that of basic anxiety, which she defined as the feeling a child has of being isolated and helpless in a potentially hostile world. A wide range of adverse factors in the environment can produce this insecurity in the child: direct or indirect domination, indifference, erratic behavior, lack of respect for the child's needs, lack of guidance, disparaging attitudes, too much admiration or its absence, and lack of warmth (Horney, 1945).

Anything that disturbs the security of the child in relation to his or her parents produces basic anxiety (Horney, 1945). To Horney, anxiety lives at the heart of every neurosis and is largely responsible for determining neurotic behavior. All neuroses are character problems and manifest themselves in behavior disturbances to which the defense against anxiety gives rise (Horney, 1937). How a character problem evolves is only of relative importance; emphasis is placed on the situations in which the character disturbances are made manifest. These situations are closely connected with the patterns of behavior by a given culture (Horney, 1945).

NEUROTIC NEEDS, TRENDS, AND SOLUTIONS

Initially, Horney presented 10 response patterns that are acquired as a consequence of trying to find solutions to disturbed interpersonal human relations (Horney, 1950). These are referred to as "neurotic needs" because they are considered irrational solutions to the problem. These 10 neurotic needs are:

1. for indiscriminate affection and approval
2. for a partner who will take over one's life
3. to restrict one's life within narrow borders
4. for power
5. to exploit others
6. for prestige
7. for personal admiration
8. for personal achievement
9. for self-sufficiency and independence
10. for perfection and unassailability

The above needs or patterns of neurotic behavior can be reduced to three groups of neurotic trends (Horney, 1945): 1. moving toward people—out of a feeling of helplessness; 2. moving away from people—also out of a feeling of helplessness; and 3. moving against people—such as having an excessive need for power. Horney contended that these three patterns exist in all individuals but exist in the neurotic in an aggravated form.

The trends break down into five neurotic solutions (Horney, 1950):

1. *The compliant neurotic character.* This type of person has a self-esteem that rises and falls with the approval he or she gets and overvalues the judgment of others.
2. *The aggressive neurotic pattern.* This individual assumes that everyone is hostile and he or she continually battles with many people.
3. *The detached character.* This person avoids all emotional interaction and places emphasis on intellectual pursuits.

4. *The idealized self-image.*   The individual cannot
   accept himself or herself unless he or she can realize
   the mandates of an unrealistic, overtaxing ego ideal.
   This person feels very vulnerable whenever he or she
   makes mistakes. His or her *real self* becomes despised
   whenever the mandates of the idealized self-image are
   not realized.
5. *Externalization.* Situational events are viewed as the
   cause of all behavior and feelings.

For Horney, psychotherapy is a human collaborative
adventure. Dogma, rules, and technique are eschewed and
emphasis is on the therapist and patient's equal partner-
ship (Hall & Lindzey, 1957). Horney's emphasis on the
social context and situational variables in diagnosis and
treatment can be well utilized by all clinicians regardless
of their theoretical preferences or preferred therapeutic
modalities. As the role of "the culture" becomes more
accepted by practitioners as they assess and treat their
patients, Horney and her concepts will probably become
more appreciated in years to come.

HARRY STACK SULLIVAN

Rejecting much of Freud, Sullivan started his own "school"
of psychoanalysis, often referred to as "the interpersonal
school of psychoanalysis."

Born in 1892, Sullivan died at the age of 57, having
contributed a great deal to psychoanalysis as a theory of
personality and treatment. From 1923 until 1930, Sullivan
was associated with the Medical School of the University
of Maryland and with the Sheppard and Enoch Pratt
Hospital in Maryland. During this time he became interested in schizophrenia and did extensive treatment with
and research on schizophrenic patients. He became very

much interested in the interpersonal behavior of his patients and brought his dedicated spirit and enthusiasm to the William Alanson White Foundation, of which he was president from 1933 to 1943, to the Washington School of Psychiatry, which he founded in 1936, and the journal *Psychiatry*, which he originated (Mullahy, 1948; Munroe, 1955).

Sullivan is well known for his view of the therapist as "a participant observer" (Sullivan, 1947). Much more than a passive observer, Sullivan viewed the therapist as a vital participant in an interpersonal situation who always has the potential to facilitate or impede communication. The therapist has his or her own apprehensions and personal problems with which to cope and which always affect the patient (Mullahy, 1948; Sullivan, 1947).

One of Sullivan's major interests was "The Interview." He conceptualized it as a system or series of systems of interpersonal processes arising from participant observation in which the interviewer derives certain conclusions about the interviewee. Sullivan (1954) divided the interview into four stages: the formal inception, reconnaissance, detailed inquiry, and termination. In an interview, according to Sullivan, there is always a great deal of reciprocity between the two parties. Sullivan's (1954) "reciprocal emotion" implies that interviewer and interviewee are continually reflecting each other's feelings.

Because all psychological dysfunctions are manifestations of faulty interpersonal processes, Sullivan concentrated on correcting the patient's perceptions of self through appropriate interpersonal processes in the therapeutic situation. To Sullivan, schizophrenic patients are not hopeless cases to be shut away in the back wards of mental institutions; they can be treated successfully if the therapist is willing to be patient, understanding, and observant (Hall & Lindzey, 1957).

SULLIVAN'S MAJOR CONCEPTS

Sullivan viewed the personality as existing only when the individual is behaving in relation to another person. Thinking, remembering, imagining, and dreaming are interpersonal because none of these processes can take place without being related to another person (Sullivan, 1947).

DYNAMISMS

A dynamism is the relatively enduring pattern of energy transformations, which recurrently characterize the organism in its duration as a living species (Sullivan, 1953). An energy transformation may be overt or covert; it is a pattern of behavior that recurs and endures, like a habit. There are dynamisms of malevolence, lust, fear, and so forth, that is, any habitual reaction towards one or more persons, whether it be in the form of a feeling, an attitude, or an overt action.

A dynamism employs a zone of the body such as the mouth, the hands, or the genitals. A zone has a *receptor* for receiving stimuli, an *effector* for performing action, and a connecting apparatus called *educators* in the central nervous system which connect the receptor mechanism with the effector mechanism (Sullivan, 1953).

Most dynamisms serve the purpose of satisfying the basic needs of the organism. One of the dynamisms, however, develops out of anxiety, namely the *self-system*. Because individuals in their interpersonal relations will be threatened by disapproval, lack of love, and other threats to their security, they adopt various types of protective measures. To avoid censure, they can conform; to avoid punishment, they may produce. These measures, called "security measures" from the self-system, sanction certain forms of behavior and forbid other types. Sullivan called these two forms the "good-me" self and the "bad-me" self (1953).

Despite the fact that a self-system is necessary, Sullivan felt it was the principal stumbling block to favorable changes in personality. Although it is the guardian of one's security, the self-system tends to become isolated from the rest of the personality (Sullivan, 1953).

PERSONIFICATIONS

A personification is an image that individuals have of themselves or of somebody else. Personifications grow out of interpersonal experiences. Therefore, the personification of a good or bad parent emanates from good or bad interpersonal experiences with them.

Personifications are rarely accurate pictures of the individuals that are being experienced. They are formed to cope with life and tend to serve an enduring type of defensive measure. Personifications that are shared by a number of people, regardless of their objectivity, are called stereotypes (Sullivan, 1947).

PROTOTAXIC, PARATAXIC, AND SYNTAXIC THINKING

Experience occurs in three modes. *Prototaxic* experience refers to the raw sensations, images, and feelings that flow through the mind. The *parataxic* type of thinking refers to causal relationships between events that occur at the same time but which are not logically related. Thus, a man gets into a car accident while wearing a green shirt and then concludes that wearing green causes accidents. The third and highest form of thinking is the *syntaxic*. This type of thinking refers to consensually validated activity, usually of a verbal nature. Words and numbers are the best examples of such thinking (Sullivan, 1953).

TENSION

Sullivan (1953) looked at the personality as an energy system whose chief work consists of activities that will reduce tension. The tension system can vary between the limits of euphoria and terror. The two main sources of tension are "anxiety" and "the needs of the organism."

STAGES OF DEVELOPMENT

In consonance with his interpersonal orientation, Sullivan (1947, 1953) conceived of maturation as essentially social. He alleged that the understanding of the growing child cannot be divorced from the youngster's social context. He postulated six stages in the development of personality.

1. The period of *infancy* extends from birth to the appearance of articulate speech. Nursing is regarded as
   an interpersonal experience and the baby, depending
   on his or her interpersonal experience of nursing,
   develops notions like "the good nipple," "the bad
   nipple," or "the wrong nipple." Other characteristics
   of the stage of infancy are apathy, somnolent detach-
   ment, movement from prototaxic to parataxic thinking, the organization of personifications, the beginning of a self-system and more autonomous functioning
   (Sullivan, 1947, 1953).
2. In *childhood*, the youngster learns language and becomes more syntaxic in his or her thinking. During
   this period the self-system becomes more coherent as
   the youngster speaks with more precision, finds play-
   mates, and develops personifications. In childhood
   the youngster recognizes that not everybody will treat
   him or her well. This is known as *malevolent transformation* (Sullivan, 1953).
3. As children enter into groups and learn the meaning
   of cooperation and competition, they develop *an
   orientation in living*, namely insight, ideals, and principles to living.
4. The need for an intimate relationship with "a chum"
   of the same sex with whom one can confide character-
   izes the late *juvenile stage*.

5. Heterosexual activity marks *early adolescence* and the lust dynamism appears. Sullivan pointed out that many of the conflicts of adolescence arise out of opposing needs for sexual gratification, security, and intimacy.
6. *Late adolescence* begins a rather extended era in which privileges, duties, satisfaction, and responsibilities in interpersonal living become salient.

SEXUALITY

Although Sullivan's interpersonal orientation reigns supreme at all times, he ascribes only a minor role to sexuality, despite its importance in interpersonal relationsips. Sullivan does not ascribe any sexual interests to the child and he denies the instinctual origin of behavior, viewing instincts as peculiarly "offensive" and "an extravagance" of language (Sullivan, 1953).

CONFLICT AND NEUROTIC SYNDROMES

For Sullivan, it is the need for security and to avoid anxiety that give rise to neurotic conflict. He has identified nine syndromes that are the result of the individual's inability to come to adequate terms with anxiety. The following personality types can be viewed as evolving for the purpose of controlling anxiety (Sullivan, 1953):

1. The completely self-absorbed type, preoccupied with wishful thinking and fantasies.
2. The psychopathic personality.
3. The "negativistic syndrome," which describes egocentric, negative types.
4. The "incorrigible" person who is hostile and considers himself or herself beyond criticism.
5. Obsessionally ambitious types.
6. Asocial types who fail to see that they have responsibilities to others. In contrast to the psychopath, asocial types have values of their own.

7. Inadequate masochistic characters.
8. Homosexuality.
9. The eternal youth who perpetually looks for an ideal but never finds it.

Sullivan was the first psychoanalyst who emphasized the interpersonal relationship between patient and therapist, thus departing from the medical model, which prescribes an unequal relationship between the healthy and wise physician and the sick, naive patient. Perhaps more than any other psychoanalyst of his time, he placed strong emphasis on the contribution of the countertransference in the treatment situation. Similar to Horney and Adler, he demonstrated that the social context can never be omitted in diagnosing and treating emotional disorders. It has been said (Mullahy, 1948) that as Freud was the prophet for the Victorian age of sexual suppression, Sullivan was the prophet for our current schizoid age, our age of unrelatedness, in which people are often strangers to one another.

WILHELM REICH

A psychoanalyst who regarded himself as an orthodox Freudian throughout most of his career, Reich's main contribution to psychoanalysis was to demonstrate that the *character* of the patient, that is, his or her habitual defenses, ego functions, and traits are the underlying basis of a symptom neurosis. In addition, he was one of the first to show how body language was a means of communicating thoughts and feelings (Reich, 1948).

REICH'S MAJOR CONCEPTS

THE FUNCTION OF THE ORGASM

Reich accords to the orgasm a position of central importance in the abreaction of every conceivable form of tension. He contended that every neurotic suffers from difficulties in the sexual sphere, usually in the form of incomplete orgasm. To Reich, a neurosis is always accompanied by a blockage of sexual expression. Whenever an individual is anxious, according to Reich, he or she inhibits his or her sexuality and an incomplete orgasm is always a sign of, as well as a result of, anxiety (Reich, 1948; Wyss, 1973).

CHARACTEROLOGY

Reich's writings within the sphere of characterology constitute his most valuable contribution to psychoanalytic theory (Wyss, 1973). Reich wrote:

> To try to explain a particular case today by demonstrating that it embodies the same mechanisms and experiences as other types of illness is no longer good enough. We must admit that our analytic literature suffers a great deal from this shortcoming (1948, p. 325).

In trying to compensate for this shortcoming, Reich took on the task of interpreting the *specificity* of a given character, viewing character traits as reaction formations and stressing the difference between these and symptoms. One of the purposes of this orientation was to analyze the compulsive character, a frequent visitor to the psychoanalyst's office. The symptoms emerge, according to Reich, because the basis of reaction—the character—is neurotic and therefore produces a libido blockage. Inasmuch as the character is the basis of the neurotic reaction, a cure can be achieved only if a character change is effected, which means that the symptom is not to be treated as the focal point of analytic work (Reich, 1948; Wyss, 1973).

The Orgone

During the last years of his life, Reich discovered the

"orgone." The orgone concept suggests that a biophysical fluid is present both in the organism and in the cosmos, concentrated in fields both around and within the organism. All the psychic processes involved in character analysis, the resolution of resistances, the interpretation of the transference, and so forth are no more than psychic descriptions of the bio-physical processes of the orgone (Reich, 1948; Wyss, 1973).

Reich's orgone theory was never taken seriously by psychoanalysts. Nonetheless, his notions on the importance of character and character analysis have earned him the respect of the psychoanalytic profession.

As Walter Briehl (1966) stated in the book, *Psychoanalytic Pioneers,*

> Notwithstanding the opinion of practically all of Reich's colleagues that he had disassociated himself from acceptable psychoanalytic theory and practice [with his notions about the orgone], there is a unanimity of opinion that his thinking and earlier works have earned a permanent place in the archives of psychoanalytic literature. (p. 437)

HEINZ HARTMANN

As psychoanalysis developed, it moved from being an "id psychology" to being more preoccupied with the ego. One of the earliest ego psychologists was Heinz Hartmann (1894–1970), a psychoanalyst steeped in Freudian tradition who tried to fulfill Freud's hope of creating a general psychoanalytic psychology. To achieve this end, psychoanalytic theories had to prove valid for both the normal and the pathological in mental life.

HARTMANN'S MAJOR CONCEPTS

CONFLICT AND CONFLICT-FREE EGO FUNCTIONS

Most of Hartmann's major contributions to ego psychology

are in his book, *Ego Psychology and the Problem of Adaptation* (1958). Here he begins the study of ego functions by noting that, although the ego grows as a result of conflict (which is what Freud posited), this is not the only root of its development. Hartmann distinguished two groups of ego functions, those specifically involved in conflict and those that develop outside of conflict—perception, thinking, memory, language, walking, and learning processes. Hartmann introduced the concept of a *conflict-free ego sphere*, which is an ensemble of functions that at any given time exert their effects outside the region of mental conflicts.

AUTONOMY

Conflict-free ego functions exist from birth and are not the result of drive modification. Their independence from drives is also characterized by their autonomous development, and for this reason Hartmann called them *primary autonomous functions* of the ego (1958). The notion of autonomy is only relative. Hartmann noted that one cannot think of an ego in isolation, without the stimulating influence of drives, the superego, and the external environment.

AVERAGE EXPECTABLE ENVIRONMENT

At birth, according to Hartmann, the human being is adapted to "an average expectable environment," a state of adaptedness that exists before the "intentional" processes of adaptation begin (Hartmann, 1964). The human being's initial adaptedness and the subsequent adaptation processes imply an interrelationship with biological and social reality.

DEVELOPMENT

Development is viewed by Hartmann as a result of the complicated interaction between instinctual drives, ego defenses, and autonomous ego functions—as a gradual unfolding of the psychic structure under the impact of processes of differentiation and integration (Hartmann, 1958, 1964).

In discussing adaptability and the processes of adaptation, Hartmann emphasized that one must consider not only early childhood but also the human's ability to maintain adaptation in later life (Hartmann, 1964).

In the life of the individual, the ego's autonomous functions are not limited to those present in early infancy. During socialization in childhood and the complex adaptations to the exigencies of society, the human being forms various behavior patterns, character structures, ego apparatuses and tendencies (Hartmann, 1958).

CHANGE OF FUNCTION

Another Hartmann (1958) concept is that in the process of development and socialization, parts of the ego which are initially involved in conflict may show a *change of function*. For example, a child may utilize part of the ego to defend against anal matters by being clean, orderly, and punctilious. These character traits, initially defenses (Reich, 1948), may eventually become part of the character and be conflict free.

Hartmann (1964) distinguished *primary autonomous ego functions*, that is, those present at birth or soon after, from *secondary autonomous ego functions*, which mature subsequently as a result of change of function. The stability of secondary autonomous zones can be measured by their resistance to regression.

NEUTRALIZATION

To describe sublimation with respect to either libido or aggression, Hartmann (1964) used the term *neutralization*.

The neutralized energy put at the disposal of the ego accounts for the secondary autonomy of some of its functions. For the ego's primary autonomous functions, Hartmann introduced the concept of *primary ego energy* (1964).

REGRESSION IN THE SERVICE OF THE EGO

In certain instances regression (play, daydreaming, fantasy) can serve creative ends and contribute to adaptation (Hartmann, 1958).

In many ways Hartmann succeeded in validating the notion that psychoanalysis can be a general psychology that can guide us in understanding both adaptive and maladaptive functioning. He also helped us to appreciate and utilize in our work as mental health professionals a more complex ego with many functions, for example, autonomous, conflict-free, adaptive, and so forth. He provided a bridge with which we can relate the person to social reality so that in diagnosing and treating patients we can integrate situational factors, intrapsychic processes, and interpersonal responses.

ANNA FREUD

As a teacher, researcher, and clinician, Anna Freud (1895–1982) is the only one of Sigmund Freud's offspring to enter the field of psychoanalysis. She is recognized in her own right as an internationally renowned psychoanalyst. Although her research and practice centered largely on the theory of child development and the psychoanalytic treatment of the child, her contributions have had implications for therapeutic work with adults as well.

Considered her father's favorite, Anna Freud always remained loyal to classical Freudian analysis. At no point in her career did she depart from Sigmund Freud's orien-

tation. Originally a teacher of young children, she rather
quickly moved toward her first love, psychoanalysis, and
is one of the world's most creative contributors to the field
of child psychoanalysis.

In addition to her extremely well-received writing,
Anna Freud's most significant contribution lies in the
organization and development of the Hampstead Child
Therapy Clinic in London, England. Numerous publications produced by Anna Freud and her colleagues concern themselves with the maturation and treatment of
children and adolescents. In all of her work there is a
constant emphasis on the direct observation of children
and the effect of this observational material on aspects
of classical psychoanalytic theory (Pumpian-Mindlin,
1966; Wolman, 1972).

Some of the studies at Hampstead were on the initial
session of children, adolescents' distrust of their therapists, children who were born blind, and on institutional-
ized children (Pumpian-Mindlin, 1966). She has
collaborated with Dorothy Burlingham (1943a; 1943b),
studying children who were orphaned early in life. Their
books, *War and Children* and *Infants Without Families*,
although published over 50 years ago, are still frequently
referred to in the analytic literature.

ANNA FREUD'S MAJOR CONCEPTS

DIAGNOSTIC EVALUATION OF CHILDREN

One of Anna Freud's major contributions is in the area of
diagnostic evaluation of children. In addition to clinical
questions involving the handling of interviews with children and the timely use of interventions, Anna Freud
developed guidelines for the assessment of pathology and
normality along developmental lines. She found that the
criteria for the assessment of pathology in adults are of

limited help in work with children. In children, symptoms present themselves in a chaotic, disorderly fashion and pathology in children manifests itself in an arrest in their development (A. Freud, 1965).

LINES OF DEVELOPMENT

In order to determine the whys and wherefores of a child's arrest, Anna Freud asserted that one must know something about the lines of development of the child. She spoke of three main categories of developmental lines: 1. *maturation* of drives and ego functions; 2. *adaptation* to the environment and to building object relations; and 3. *organization*, the integration and conflicts within the psychic structure (A. Freud, 1965; Pumpian-Mindlin, 1966).

Anna Freud referred to the necessity of laying down guidelines for what the clinician can expect at any particular age of a child, both in terms of accomplishments, conflicts, and difficulties. She called attention to the progressive and regressive swings in the development of the child and helped the clinician realize that pathology in children is not assessed simply on the basis of whether a particular symptom is present or absent. Rather, what Anna Freud has demonstrated is that a comprehensive evaluation of a child requires a thorough assessment of the degree of harmony or disharmony along the various developmental lines in relation to the forces of both ego and id. With this more flexible evaluation of child development at different stages, what results is a greater tolerance for individual variation within the limits of normality and for progressive and regressive swings in the individual (Wolman, 1972).

Much of Anna Freud's research was an attempt to pinpoint how much of childhood behavior that was regarded as maladaptive at one time in the child's development is "par for the course" at another time. The child's behavior as such cannot be termed pathological unless one takes into consideration the child's stage of development at the time he or she is being diagnostically evaluated (A. Freud, 1965).

Anna Freud stated that there is one basic developmental line that has received attention from psychoanalysts from the beginning and that can serve as the prototype for all others. This is the sequence that leads from the newborn's utter dependence on maternal care to the young adult's emotional self-reliance (A. Freud, 1965).

THE EGO AND THE MECHANISMS OF DEFENSE

Anna Freud (1946) was the first psychoanalyst to provide a comprehensive account of the ego's defense mechanisms vis-à-vis the id, the superego, and the outside world. In her well-known book *The Ego and the Mechanisms of Defense* (1946), to which we have referred several times, Anna Freud emphasized the role of the ego as the "seat of observation." In order for the individual to cope with the anxiety that is stimulated by instinctual wishes that are unacceptable to the ego or responding to the superego's commands or to threats from the external world, Anna Freud suggested that the individual employs one or more of the defense mechanisms we reviewed in Chapter 1— repression, reaction formation, projection, and so forth.

EQUIDISTANCE

The notion that the "good" therapist stays equidistant from id, ego, and superego is one of Anna Freud's very helpful contributions to therapy. By equidistant she suggested that the analyst does not champion id wishes or reinforce superego commands—he or she exposes all parts of the patient's psyche to him or her without imposing value to any psychic agency (A.Freud, 1946).

Anna Freud will always be remembered as an outstanding researcher, lucid writer, able clinician, and a founder of child psychoanalysis. More than any other analyst she helped clinicians appreciate the dangers that make defenses necessary as well as the purposes they serve.

ERIK ERIKSON

A colleague of Anna Freud's who worked at Hampstead, Erik Erikson, after graduating from the Vienna Psychoanalytic Institute, came to the United States in the 1930s and for much of his career has been a professor of human development and psychiatry at Harvard University. Erikson is the author of a series of major, prize-winning works including *Childhood and Society* (1950), *Identity and the Life Cycle* (1959), and *Insight and Responsibility* (1964).

ERIKSON'S MAJOR CONCEPTS

In *Childhood and Society* (1950), Erikson formulated his epigenetic ground plan, suggesting that the child's development can never be understood without knowing a great deal about the youngster's "radius of significant others." Significant others aid, abet, or hinder the organism's coping with and resolving specific life tasks.

In demonstrating that the human being not only unfolds according to predetermined phases from its biological beginnings (oral, anal, phallic, oedipal stages) but also constantly interacts with an environment, he expanded Freud's stages of psychosexual development into eight stages of the life cycle—an orientation used by many mental health professionals.

THE EIGHT STAGES

1. *Basic trust versus basic mistrust.* This initial stage, occurring during the first year of life, is the period when the child's basic attitude toward himself or herself is acquired. If the infant's basic needs are met

and discomforts are attended to, the infant will develop an inner certainty and a sense of basic trust, which is regarded by Erikson as being the cornerstone of the healthy personality.

2. *Autonomy versus shame and doubt.* With the maturation of the muscular system, retentive and eliminative modes come to the fore at the second stage of what Erikson views as "the battle of autonomy." Erikson regards this stage to be decisive for the ratio between love and hate, freedom of self-expression, or its suppression. The overly controlled child capitulates to the tyrannical social reality, and shame and doubt are evoked within the psyche.

3. *Initiative versus guilt.* As children move about more efficiently, as language develops, and locomotion expands, their imagination increases, and eventually they become preoccupied with future role and sex differences. This stage with its consuming curiosity is marked by genital excitability and fantasy.

   If the environment can accept the child's burgeoning sexual development and curiosity, he or she can successfully take initiative in interpersonal and other activity. If not, guilt and a restrictive mode of approaching reality can result.

4. *Industry versus inferiority.* Here, school becomes the focus of much of the child's life, and performance is crucial to further socialization. The child needs to find the tools, skills, and roles that will permit identification with others on a more socialized level. If children can develop skills that their culture prizes and are initiated into roles that their culture provides, then they have mastered a life task that is of vital importance for future work and social relationships.

   If the environment contains appropriate role models such as teachers and peers, the child gains a sense of industry and achievement.

5. *Identity versus identity diffusion.* This stage occurs during adolescence and Erikson sees the crucial task at this juncture to be the quest for identity that will anchor the youth's transcient existence in the here-and-now. By ego identity, Erikson means the accrued confidence that one's ability to maintain inner sameness and continuity is matched by the sameness and continuity of one's meaning for others.

   The social task of this stage is settling on a vocational or professional identity. To keep themselves intact pending the arrival of a sense of identity, adolescents frequently overidentify with movie heroes, athletes, and other "ideals." Tight affiliation with the in-group and intolerance for different styles and behavior are defensive maneuvers the adolescent utilizes to cope with the lack of a stable feeling of identity.

6. *Intimacy versus isolation.* If there has been an establishment of identity in adolescence, the young adult can move toward an intimate relationship with the opposite sex. A stable sexual identity helps the young man or woman feel pleasure in sharing with and caring for another without the fear of losing himself or herself.

   The danger in this period is that of self-isolation— the avoidance of contacts that will lead to interpersonal and/or sexual intimacy because of a threat of loss of identity.

7. *Generativity versus stagnation.* At this stage of development the positive sense to be acquired is generativity, the concern in establishing and guiding the next generation. Although altruistic concern and creativity are seen as alternatives, Erikson's main concern here is the sense of mastery and pleasure in guiding one's offspring.

   Should the adult not be able to invest in the younger

generation, stagnation and psychological ill health ensues.

8. *Ego integrity versus despair.* By ego integrity, Erikson means self-acceptance and valuing one's life-style. It is the culmination of resolving successfully the previous life stages. Despair colors the life and psyche of one who is devoid of integrity.

Erikson's explication of the eight stages of man concerns itself with the "normal" child and adult. Each stage may be aggravated by a poor coordination between the individual and his or her environment. Then, the ratio of a negative ego state to a positve one can be quite high and mistrust can become more dominant than trust; self-doubt can assume a higher proportion in the person than autonomy.

In addition to a life task being incompletely resolved, individuals can regress to earlier stages when current life tasks are overwhelming.

Each item in Erikson's eight stages should not be regarded as a discrete unit but each is needed for a healthy personality. For example, in order to develop a coherent sense of "autonomy," the individual has to "trust" first.

The eight stages have often been called eight "crises" to connote not a threat of catastrophe but a turning point and a crucial period of increased vulnerabilty and heightened potential.

In utilizing Erikson's notions in therapy (Strean, 1975), the role of the clinician can be conceptualized as helping the patient resolve a current life task by offering those emotional and interpersonal experiences that are necessary to help the patient resolve a particular life task and thereby move up the psychosocial ladder.

The eminent psychologist, David Rappoport (1960) repeatedly affirmed his view that Erikson's concepts fit broadly into the conceptual framework of psychoanalysis and furnish "for the first time a theory and an epigenetic ground plan of ego development" (p. 136).

MELANIE KLEIN

As one of the foremost clinicians and researchers in the history of child psychoanalysis, Melanie Klein influenced countless numbers of therapists who work with children and adults. Early in her career she tried interpreting to children in play therapy what Freud did with the dreams of adults. She attracted—and continues to attract— many followers and dissenters, as she attempted to modify Freud's theories on personality development and treatment.

Born in 1882 in Vienna, Melanie Klein studied art and history. However, her first love was psychoanalysis to which she became attached when she was in her mid-20s and remained devoted until her death in 1960.

KLEIN'S MAJOR CONCEPTS

CHILD ANALYSIS

Klein was convinced that with the child one can achieve an analytic relationship free from educational, moral, or reassuring interferences, in which a proper analysis can be carried out. She noted that all therapists who begin to work with children find, to their surprise, that even in very young children the capacity for insight is far greater than in adults. She believed that the connections between the conscious and the unconscious are closer in young children than in adults, that infantile repressions are less powerful, and that the infant's intellectual capacities are often underrated (Lindon, 1966).

VIEW OF THE SUPEREGO

From her work with children, Klein became convinced

that the superego begins in early infancy, in contrast to
Freud's notion that it is the "heir to the Oedipus complex"
and shows itself at about age 3. Klein contended that the
young toddler experiences the superego as a variety of
figures that actually function within the toddler's body.
These internal figures were once external objects that are
later introjected. In studying the superego, Klein discovered the vital part that reparation plays in mental life and
believed that reparation includes the variety of processes
by which the ego undoes harm done in fantasy and re-
stores, preserves, and revives objects (Klein & Riviere,
1937; Lindon, 1966).

ANXIETY

In her analysis of children and adults, Klein concluded
that anxiety of a psychotic nature is part of normal infantile development. These psychotic paranoid and depressive anxieties are transient but universal (Klein, 1932;
Segal, 1964).

SYMBOLS

In her work with children in play therapy, Klein concluded that symbolism enabled the child to transfer not
only objects but fantasies, anxieties, and guilt to objects
other than people. Klein believed that in children a severe
inhibition of the capacity to form and use symbols and
develop a fantasy life is a sign of serious disturbance
(Lindon, 1966).

PSYCHOANALYSIS OF CHILDREN

In her book *The Psychoanalysis of Children*, Klein (1932)
posits that the Oedipus complex begins in the first year of
life (not the third, as Freud contended); that part of
development in the first and second years of life is an
inevitable depression when the youngster feels separate

from the mother; and that a little later the child finds himself or herself in the "paranoid-schizoid" position, a point of fixation in psychotic illness. Klein also contended that envy begins in the first year of life.

INTROJECTION AND PROJECTION

In her analysis of children, Klein saw introjection and projection constantly at work. She asserted that introjection and projection function from the beginning of postnatal life. Introjection implies that the outer world is experienced as taken into the self and becomes part of the infant's inner life. Projection is a process whereby the infant attributes to other people around him or her feelings that operate within. Love and hate toward the mother are bound up with the infant's capacity to project all emotions onto her, thereby making her a good and bad object (Klein & Riviere, 1937; Lindon, 1966; Segal, 1964).

SPLITTING

According to Klein another of the activities of the infantile mind is "splitting," which is the tendency to separate impulses and objects into various aspects, good and bad, damaged and undamaged. This occurs because the early ego lacks coherence and because persecutory anxieties reinforce the need to keep the loved object separate from the dangerous one, thereby leading to a splitting of love from hate (Lindon, 1966; Segal, 1964).

PROJECTIVE IDENTIFICATION

Allied with splitting is projective identification. This involves the splitting off of those qualities of one's own mind that are experienced as dangerous, and projecting them onto some other person, and then identifying with that person (Segal, 1964).

Although Melanie Klein has always been a controver-

sial psychoanalyst, frequently at odds with Anna Freud
and other mainstream Freudians, her creativity and dedi-
cation have been acknowledged by those who knew her
and are familiar with her work. Several prominent analysts such as Bion (1955), Fairbairn (1952), and Grotstein
(1966), who are regarded as Kleinians, have expanded on
her theories and keep Melanie Klein very much alive in the
analytic world.

DONALD W. WINNICOTT

An English pediatrician who became an outstanding child
analyst, Winnicott was born in 1896 and died in 1971.
Concomitant with his pediatric work and child analysis,
Winnicott treated very disturbed adult patients. This
work often entailed a "phase of management" of a disturbed patient who had "regressed to dependency." These
patients required a period of steady emotions, "holding"
rather than interpretive work before analytic work could
begin. Through this work, Winnicott came to see the
importance of his own behavior apart from his function
as an interpreter of conflict (Moore and Fine, 1990;
Winnicott, 1971b).

WINNICOTT'S MAJOR CONCEPTS

GOOD-ENOUGH MOTHER

A good-enough mother is one who offers a holding environment that provides an optimal amount of constancy
and comfort for the infant who is wholly dependent on her
(Winnicott, 1971b).

HOLDING

This is a maternal provision that organizes a facilitative
environment which the dependent infant needs. Holding
refers to the natural skill and constancy of the good-
enough mother (Moore & Fine, 1990; Winnicott, 1971b).

PLAYING

Play extends the dialogue between the feeding infant and the mother through the use of toys and other playthings. Play is an ego activity, according to Winnicott, only minimally invested with libidinal or aggressive energy (Winnicott, 1971a).

POTENTIAL SPACE

This is an area of mutual creativity that occurs between an infant and the mother. For example, the mother may introduce a toy or some other object to the infant at the right time, so that mother and child spontaneously interact as the child learns more about his or her environment (Winicott, 1971a).

PRECURSOR OBJECT

Inanimate objects offered by the mother, or parts of the child's or mother's body, are objects that the child mouths and uses for consolation. The child may use his or her tongue, hair, fingers, pacifier, or bottle in this way (Moore & Fine, 1990; Winnicott, 1971b).

PRIMARY CREATIVITY

As the earliest manifestations and primal origins of the child's creative capacity, primary creativity refers to the capacity to view the world in a creative way and to play (Moore & Fine, 1990; Winnicott, 1971a).

PRIMARY MATERNAL PREOCCUPATION

This is a maternal state of mind that Winnicott saw as a "healthy illness." It begins before the baby is born and continues for several weeks after birth; the mother is deeply if not solely preoccupied with the infant (Winnicott, 1971b).

TRANSITIONAL OBJECT

This is the infant's first "not-me" possession, something inanimate but valued (often a soft blanket or toy), which the child uses in the course of emotional separation from the mother; the transitional object is often used going to sleep and at times of stress (Winnicott, 1958).

TRUE SELF, FALSE SELF

The *true self* is the inherited potential that constitutes the "kernel" of the child. Its continuing development and establishment are facilitated by a good-enough mother who provides a healthy environment and a meaningful responsiveness to the very young infant's sensorimotor and postural self. Winnicott viewed the true self as closer to the spontaneous representation of the id (Winnicott, 1965).

A *false self* indicates the absence of a true self, usually in a schizoid individual. If the mother is unable to meet the "id" self of the infant, and imposes herself and her own needs on the youngster, a false self emerges (Winnicott, 1965).

In summing up Winnicott's work, Moore and Fine (1990) state:

> His imaginative contributions to the theory and practice of psychoanalysis stand against the background of a long career in which he remained an exponent of psychoanalysis as a rigorous undertaking, the main instrument of which was interpretation within a context of silent and careful observation. (p. 205)

HEINZ KOHUT

An elaboration of concepts of narcissism and the self was developed by Heinz Kohut and his colleagues. Born in 1913, Kohut for many years was a classical Freudian medical analyst. In the early 1970s he modified his orientation and founded Self Psychology. Self Psychology recognizes as the most fundamental essence of human psychology the individual's needs to organize his or her psyche into a cohesive configuration, the self, and to establish self-sustaining relationships between this self and its surroundings that maintain coherence, vigor, and balanced harmony among its parts (Moore & Fine, 1990).

KOHUT'S MAJOR CONCEPTS

Kohut's major concepts have appeared in several of his books: *The Analysis of the Self* (1971); *The Restoration of the Self* (1977); and *The Search for the Self* (1978). Kohut died in 1981 but his Self Psychology is very much alive and a very popular "school" of psychoanalysis.

THE SELF

The self refers to the nuclear core of the personality. It is made up of various constituents that emerge into a coherent and enduring configuration through the interplay of heredity and environment. Constituents of the self are (1) the pole from which basic strivings for admiration and recognition emanate; (2) the pole that maintains the guiding ideals; and (3) the arc of tension between the two poles that activates the basic talents and skills (Kohut, 1971, 1977).

SELF TYPES

Inasmuch as the self has different attributes depending on its level of development, various self types have been described. Some of them are the following: The *virtual self* refers to the image of the neonate's self as it resides in the parent's mind. The *nuclear self* is the nascent organization that emerges as a cohesive structure in the second year of life. The *cohesive self* is the relatively coherent structure of the normal and healthily functioning self. The *grandiose self* is the normal, early infantile, exhibitionistic self dominated by omnipotent desires (Kohut, 1971, 1977, 1978; Moore & Fine, 1990).

PATHOLOGICAL SELF STATES

The *archaic self* is a pathological condition in which the nuclear self-configuration of early childhood dominates adult functioning. The *fragmenting self* is a chronic state of the self characterized by diminished coherence. The *empty self* is a depressed self without vigor (Kohut, 1971, 1977).

THE SELFOBJECT

This is one's subjective experience of another person who provides a sustaining function to the self within a relationship, evoking and maintaining the self by his or her presence or activity, for example, a loving mother. Though the term is applied to the participating persons in the individual's social orbit, it is used mainly to describe the intrapsychic experience of various types of relationships between the self and others (Kohut, 1991; Moore & Fine, 1990).

SELF DISORDERS

Psychosis is characterized by serious, permanent or protracted damages to the self with no effective defensive structure to cover the defect. *Borderline states* also involve serious, permanent damage to the self, but defenses can protect the person from going psychotic. *Narcissistic behavior disorders* are temporary damages to the self but are responsive to psychoanalytic treatment (Moore & Fine, 1990). However, Kohut (1971, 1977) contended that psychoses and borderline states are not usually responsive to psychoanalytic treatment.

SELFOBJECT TRANSFERENCE

This is the displacement onto the analyst of the patient's need for a responsive selfobject matrix. This term has replaced the term *narcissistic transference* (Moore & Fine, 1990).

MIRROR TRANSFERENCE

This refers to the recapitulation within the treatment situation of a wish for acceptance, approval, and confirmation of the self by the selfobject matrix to strengthen the damaged pole of ambitions. It is manifested by demands on the analyst for recognition, admiration, and praise (Kohut, 1978).

IDEALIZING TRANSFERENCE

This transference exists when the wish for idealization or merger with a strong and wise selfobject is reestablished in order to strengthen the damaged pole of ideals (Kohut, 1971, 1977).

TWINSHIP TRANSFERENCE

This occurs when an early, reassuring latency or prelatency experience is reestablished. It represents the need to see and understand as well as to be seen and be understood by someone like oneself (Kohut, 1977; Moore & Fine, 1990).

MERGER TRANSFERENCE

This merger represents the reestablishment of an archaic identity with the selfobject of childhood through an extension of the self to include the analyst. In *transference of creativity*, there is a transient need of certain creative personalities for merger with a selfobject while engaged in a difficult creative task (Kohut, 1978; Moore & Fine, 1990).

Throughout all of Kohut's writings is a strong emphasis on the growing child's need as well as on the patient's need for empathy. In Reppen's (1985) book *Beyond Freud*, Kohut's emphasis on the crucial importance of empathy is viewed as his major contribution to psychoanalytic theory and practice.

RECOMMENDED READINGS

For comprehensive bibliographies on some of the leading psychoanalysts throughout history, see *Psychoanalytic Pioneers*, edited by Alexander, Eisenstein, and Grotjahn. In addition to valuable personal data on the psychoanalytic pioneers, some of their major concepts are reviewed.

An interesting attempt to show how the psychodynamics of the theorist relate to his theory may be found in *Faces in a Cloud: Subjectivity in Personality Theory* by Stolorow and Atwood. Here, the dynamics and major concepts of Freud, Rank, Reich, and Jung are considered. In *Personality Theory and Social Work Practice*, Strean shows how social work practice can be enhanced by incorporating some of the concepts of Freud, Rank, Horney, Sullivan, A. Freud, Hartmann, and other psychoanalysts.

For excellent summaries and discussions of the major concepts of more modern psychoanalysts such as Kohut, Bion, and other analysts not mentioned in this chapter, for example, Kernberg, Mahler, and Lacan, see *Beyond Freud* by Joseph Reppen.

Psychoanalytic Terms and Concepts by Moore and Fine has excellent summaries on the conceptualizations of Klein, Kohut, Bion, Winnicott, and Jung.

Hall and Lindzey in *Theories of Personality* have reviewed the life and contributions of Freud, Jung, Adler, Horney, Sullivan, and Fromm.

Wyss's *Psychoanalytic Schools* in an excellent resource for information on the major modifiers of Freud's theories.

3

A PSYCHOANALYTIC PERSPECTIVE ON PSYCHOPATHOLOGY

INTRAPSYCHIC CONFLICT

Psychoanalytically oriented practitioners and theorists contend that psychological conflicts are part of the human condition (Hartmann, 1958). Conflicts, they allege, are inevitable, universal, and one of the most important dynamic factors underlying human behavior. Psychoanalysts believe that the outcome of intrapsychic conflict determines the basis of all of our behavior and attitudes— adaptive and maladaptive, normal and abnormal, neurotic and psychotic.

But what is intrapsychic conflict? As we discussed in Chapter 1, there is a constant struggle between the structures of the psyche, id, ego, and superego. This struggle is what we mean by intrapsychic conflict. In Chapter 1 we gave an example of "normal" intrapsychic conflict when we referred to the struggle most of us experience when the alarm clock goes off in the morning. The id wish to sleep conflicts with the superego command to get up; the ego then mediates the struggle and tries to effect a compromise between the demands of the psychic structures and those from the outside world. If the decision does not involve coping with too much anxiety, the conflict will be resolved fairly easily and quickly. However, if strong id wishes conflict sharply with prohibitive superego demands and/ or with the demands of the external world, we may experience intense anxiety. We may develop a neurotic symptom such as an obsession, a compulsion, a phobia, or even a psychotic reaction in which we may become acutely paranoid. Thus, when the alarm clock goes off, we may arise from bed with only a minimum of resistance. But, instead, we could obsess over the decision for half an hour or more while we lie in bed. Or we might compulsively stare at the clock for a long time as we roll and toss in bed but do not get up. Then, too, we may become paralyzed, stay in bed, and gratify the id wishes to rest but have strong fantasies that our boss is downstairs with a gun ready to shoot us because we resist working!

Because conflicts are part of the human condition, the differences between normal, neurotic, and psychotic behavior are always a matter of degree. The main difference between a neurotic reaction (or something more severe) and an adaptive response is that the anxiety aroused by the id wishes cannot be controlled by defenses such as projection and denial, and a symptom develops to bind the anxiety.

Anxiety is always a warning for the person that some unacceptable wish, thought, fantasy, or memory will reach consciousness (Freud, 1923). If the unacceptable element is very strong and/or the defense against it is weak, much anxiety erupts and the individual forms a neurotic symptom. A neurotic symptom expresses simultaneously the individual's desire to express what is forbidden and the dread of that expression. In a phobia, for example a dread of going out on the street, two variables are at work. The very situation that the individual fears also excites him or her. The stimulation of fantasies that going out on the street induces, activates anxiety because the excitement emanates from sexual fantasies in the id that the superego forbids.

A symptom is often referred to as a "compromise formation" because it is a composite expression of the individual's wishes, anxiety, defenses, and fears (Brenner, 1955).

The Sequence of Intrapsychic Conflict

The formation of intrapsychic conflict works in a predictable sequence: id wishes come into conflict with internal prohibitions (superego) and/or external ones; the ego is threatened and produces anxiety to signal that a danger is imminent. Defenses are mobilized and conflict is resolved via neurotic or psychotic symptoms, character change, or adaptive behavior. Let us look at the sequence of events in a neurotic conflict of an adolescent girl:

> Annabelle, a 19-year-old university student, reported to her counselor at the student mental health service that she could not concentrate on her schoolwork because she had constant thoughts (obsessions) that her mother was dying. In addition, Annabelle had developed a compulsion in which she had to check dozens of times a day whether or not she had flushed the toilet.
>
> As Annabelle became involved in treatment, she shared with her counselor how very angry she was to be away from home. She missed the constant admiration and affection from her mother that was part of her daily life. However, what Annabelle and her counselor learned was that Annabelle was busy fighting her strong dependency wishes, her anger, and her punctured narcissism. Annabelle's defenses of repression and denial were not strong enough to cope with the

anxiety emanating from her intense dependency yearnings and her strong anger. Thus she developed a "compromise formation"—an obsessive thought. The obsessive thought expressed her deep dependency wishes for her mother and her wish to kill her mother—both forbidden id wishes that conflicted with Annabelle's strong superego prohibitions.

Annabelle's wish "to shit and piss" all over her mother, and her dread of these ideas, were expressed in her compulsion to check constantly to see if the toilet was flushed. She wanted to "mess up" her mother and also get rid of the idea at the same time. Her enormous ambivalence between messing and being clean, respecting and demeaning, emerged in a compulsion.

ROOTS OF A PSYCHONEUROSIS

Freud never abandoned the idea that the roots of a psychoneurosis lie in a disturbance of the libidinal life of childhood. He recognized rather early in his career (Freud, 1905) that sexual interests and activities, far from being limited in childhood to exceptional events, are a normal part of human psychic life from earliest infancy.

In his research on psychoneurosis, Freud compared a symptom to a dream in that both are compromise formulations of one or more repressed impulses and those forces of the personality that oppose the entrance of forbidden impulses into consciousness. Freud was also able to demonstrate that neurotic symptoms, like the elements of a dream, had a unique meaning; symptoms could be shown to be the disguised and distorted expressions of unconscious fantasies (Freud, 1900, 1905, 1923).

By permitting a partial and disguised emergence of an id

wish through a neurotic symptom, for example, Annabelle's obsessional thoughts about her mother dying, the ego is able to avoid some of the anxiety it would otherwise develop. By permitting an impulse a fantasied gratification (as in a dream) that is distorted and disguised, the ego can avoid the displeasure of experiencing extreme anxiety (Brenner, 1955). By coping with her unacceptable thoughts through an obsession and a compulsion, Annabelle was able to ward off her murderous wishes, her deep dependency yearnings, her anxiety, and her guilt. This is what is known as the *primary gain* (Freud, 1926) of a neurosis, that is, warding off dangerous impulses, thoughts, and fantasies from consciousness.

Secondary gain (Freud, 1926) refers to the efforts of the ego to exploit the gratifying possibilities of a neurotic symptom. For example, an adult with a street phobia may enjoy the luxury of being forced to stay at home and not work because going to work activates too much pain.

It is important to emphasize again that the differences between the "normal" person and the neurotic individual (or psychotic) are always ones of degree. All individuals have id wishes that are not acceptable to them. When defenses, which all individuals use, are not strong enough to cope with forbidden impulses, anxiety erupts and symptoms appear. The differences between Annabelle in the above example and other freshmen who are homesick are very minimal compared to their many similarities.

PSYCHOSES, NEUROSES, CHARACTER PROBLEMS, AND OTHER FORMS OF PSYCHOPATHOLOGY

Before we describe various forms of psychopathology such as schizophrenia, anxiety hysteria, the obsessive compulsive character, and alcoholism from a psychoanalytic point of view, it is important to first mention some of the limitations of clinical labels. To call a patient "neurotic" or "psychotic" fails to individualize him or her, does not tell us very much about the subjective suffering the patient endures, nor does it inform us much about the disruptive effects on the patient's internal and interpersonal functioning. A clinical label rarely tells us much about the strength of specific ego functions (reality testing, judgment, frustration tolerance, defenses, object relations, impulse control), the drives, and little about the rigidity or flexibility of the patient's superego. The label contains limited information about the patient's unique psychodynamics and offers few clues regarding the etiology of his or her stresses.

Clinical labels such as "borderline," "character disorder," or "psychopath" often stigmatize a patient. Consequently, some psychoanalytically oriented clinicians have rejected this form of diagnostic assessment altogether, contending that clinical labels are frequently used in the service of the therapist's negative countertransference (Fine, 1982).

Despite the aforementioned caveats, what psychoanalysts have to say about psychopathological states that confront all mental health professionals may have some utility in better understanding certain dimensions of their patients' difficulties and in planning more effective treatment strategies.

Schizophrenia

The etiology of schizophrenia continues to be debated among mental health professionals. Some contend that the dysfunction is strictly a constitutional and biological phenomenon and if treated it should chiefly be by drugs; others view schizophrenia as evolving from faulty interpersonal experiences and therefore can be treated by psychotherapy, which is a new and corrective interpersonal experience for the patients.

These two approaches have been debated for over 60 years. In 1917 Kraepelin, then the world's leading authority on schizophrenia, alleged that 70% of schizophrenic patients were incurable and if treatment could cure them, it would have to be exclusively through organic means (Kraepelin, 1917). About a decade later Harry Stack Sullivan (1931) performed an astounding job with schizophrenic patients at the Shepard and Enoch Pratt Hospital near Baltimore. Of 78 patients with acute schizophrenia he was able to show improvement in 61% of them "with a modified form of psychoanalysis.... In a considerable number the change has amounted to a recovery from the mental disorder" (Sullivan, 1931, p. 238).

Although there is not unanimity on the subject, most psychoanalytically oriented practitioners, while not denying the role of constitutional and biological factors, believe that schizophrenia is a maturational problem deriving from negative interpersonal experiences early in life.

In 1937 Freud in his paper "Analysis Terminable and Interminable" stated:

> Every normal person, in fact, is only normal on the average. His ego approximates to that part of the psychotic in some part or other and to a greater or lesser extent. (p. 235)

There is now abundant literature affirming the notion that schizophrenic patients have been deprived of normal physical and emotional stimulation during their first year of life (Brenner, 1955; Fine, 1989; Searles, 1978; Strean, 1989). Consequently, many of their ego functions have failed to develop and their capacity to relate to others is severely impaired (Fenichel, 1945). They distort reality, are plagued by murderous fantasies, which they often project onto others, and conclude that others are out to persecute them. Convinced that most people are enemies, they become seclusive, sometimes talking only to themselves.

Although there are differences in the degree of depar-
ture from reality among schizophrenic patients, they all
tend to resemble the narcissistic infant. In many ways
their egos have returned to their original undifferentiated
state and have dissolved almost entirely into the id, which
has no real knowledge of people and reality (Fenichel,
1945).

Schizophrenic patients, although suffering from large
quantities of murderous rage, tend to repress it and feel like
guilty and unworthy children. By withdrawing their
libido from other people and by directing it inward, they
feel estranged, depersonalized, and preoccupied with bodily
sensations. The regression to or fixation at the infantile
narcissistic state accounts for their megalomania. They
have either lost or never gained a basic sense of trust and
therefore have to resort to a paranoid orientation to the
world. Their thinking falls back from the logical to the
prelogical and they are consumed by archaic wishes that
give rise to hallucinatory and delusional thinking
(Erikson, 1950).

Earlier we pointed out that in neuroses two steps must
be distinguished: (1) repression (or denial, projection, and
so forth) of an id impulse; and (2) its return in a distorted
form as in an obsession or some other neurotic symptom.
In schizophrenia there are two analogous steps: (1) a break
with reality; and (2) an attempt to regain the lost reality
(Strean, 1979).

In the most comprehensive and humane treatment of the
schizophrenic patient written to date, Karon and Vandenbos
(1981), psychoanalytically oriented clinicians, point out
that in every case of schizophrenia they have treated (and
there have been hundreds of cases), "the individual had
lived a life that we could not conceive of living without
developing his symptoms. In not one case was a genetic
factor or a physiological factor needed to account for the
symptoms" (p. 40). They further state: "All of the symp-

toms of schizophrenia may be understood, however, as attempts to deal with terror (anxiety seems too mild a term) of a chronic kind. Human beings do not tolerate chronic terror well" (p. 42). Finally the authors assert, "There is nothing in the schizophrenic reactions which you will not find in the potentiality of all human beings. Any of us can and will develop so-called schizophrenic symptoms under enough stress of the right kind" (p. 42).

Manic-Depressive Psychoses

Although individuals suffering from manic-depressive psychoses are similar to schizophrenic patients in their extreme narcissism and loss of many ego functions, the unique characteristic of these individuals is their rapid alteration of moods. Within a short period of time they can shift from acute depression to intense joy—as if they are at one moment extremely helpless, agitated, and depressed infants who have lost their mothers (and therefore the whole world) only to be transformed the next moment into extremely happy children who have been reunited with their mothers.

The above description suggests some of the etiology of manic-depressive psychoses. The mood swings of the patients who suffer from it seem to mirror a situation in which the baby is alternately abandoned and loved intensely, only to be abandoned again. Manic-depressive patients appear to be the products of very unpredictable environments that offered much pain but intermittent pleasure.

> Mr. Brown, a 32-year-old patient in a mental hospital, diagnosed as suffering from manic-depressive psychosis, left his room in a crying, agitated, depressed mood to go to breakfast. As he arrived at the hospital cafeteria, instead of crying, talking about suicide, and feeling the

> world was coming to an end, he began to laugh
> and was very jovial. He ate his breakfast heartily
> and then as he left the cafeteria, his world shifted
> dramatically. Mr. Brown became depressed again
> and walked with his head lowered as if saying to
> himself, "Nobody cares about me."

Usually the jovial state of the manic-depressive during
the manic phase is accompanied by exaggerated self-love
and a flight of ideas and actions. It is as if the patient is
desperately holding onto a joyful state but wondering
when the mother's comfort will be withdrawn and the joy
destroyed (Glover, 1949).

In the depressive phase of manic-depressive psychoses,
one can usually see that these patients have suffered
decisive narcissistic injuries. They often have agitated
crying jags and appear like young children who are very
disappointed in their parents for not being available to
them (Fenichel, 1945).

The manic-depressive patient seems to be alternating
between hunger and satiety continually. Pleasure is ex-
pected after every pain, and pain after every pleasure. The
primitive idea that any suffering should be rewarded by joy
and every joy should be punished by suffering is enter-
tained continually (Glover, 1949).

Manic-depressive psychoses are often referred to as a
bipolar disorder (Moore & Fine, 1990) by those who view
the disease as primarily physiological. However, most
psychoanalysts believe the condition is triggered by loss or
personal defeat in a patient who experienced severe and
traumatic separations during childhood (Jacobson, 1953).

Some psychoanalytically oriented therapists have been
influenced by those current clinicians and researchers
who maintain that manic-depressive psychoses are exclusively biological and should be treated solely by pharma-

ceuticals. This is the view of a current popular book, *Understanding Depression: A Complete Guide to Its Diagnosis and Treatment*, by two psychiatry professors, Donald Klein and Paul Wender (1993).

Some practitioners are moving toward a notion that perhaps there are two different manic-depressive conditions, one primarily psychological, the other primarily physiological. The fact that some of these patients respond well to psychotherapy and others only to medication tends to support this hypothesis for some (Moore & Fine, 1990). However, the manic-depressive individual is often a very negative person, and his or her negative therapeutic reaction to psychotherapy does not necessarily imply that the problem or its treatment is biological.

Borderline States

Individuals with weak ego functions who relate at a low level of psychosexual development, that is, like a narcissistic infant, but have not departed from reality, are referred to as borderline personalities or as suffering from borderline states. Although these individuals suffer from the extreme narcissism, powerful feelings of omnipotence, lack of genuine object relatedness, and poor judgment associated with psychosis, they usually have some ego functions that are working well, at least at certain times. They are similar to the schizophrenic and manic-depressive patients in that much aggression pervades their psyches. These individuals are potential psychotics; they have not broken with reality, but under circumstances of acute stress, for example combat in military service, poverty, or illness, they can become psychotic (Fenichel, 1945; Glover, 1949).

Kaufman (1958) has pointed out that the "borderline personality" can be characterized as having (1) many overt depressions; (2) an inability to handle the day-to-day realities of living; (3) a tendency to act out in delinquency, alcoholism, or drug addiction; (4) psychosomatic reactions, such as ulcerative colitis; and (5) paranoid reactions. Kaufman has further noted that borderline personalities use a great deal of magical thinking. If they get into difficulty, they believe that a parental figure will come and rescue them and take care of them indefinitely.

The borderline personality usually has much difficulty coping with omnipotent fantasies and vacillates between believing that he or she can control the world and that some omnipotent person is around who will take care of every crisis in the person's life (Knight, 1953a). These patients often believe that if they act in an aggressive and hostile manner they will be more respected. Very often their hostility and aggression serve as a defense against depression and a yearning for love.

> Clara Cooley, a 40-year-old patient in psychotherapy, was kept waiting by her therapist for a minute or two before her appointment. Before she was in the therapist's office, Clara attacked the therapist, calling him "an insensitive, inconsiderate, selfish pig." She went on to say that she regretted coming for her appointment and was seriously thinking of quitting therapy altogether and felt very misunderstood.
>
> Clara, who had a very depressed mother who was not available to her very much during her childhood, had a strong desire to be held and hugged. To cope with her strong dependency yearnings that often felt unbearable, she handled her interpersonal relations with a pseudo-aggressive attitude, as if she did not want to be loved. Her indifference masked her deep hunger for human contact.

In *Current and Historical Perspectives on the Borderline*

Patient, Fine (1989) concludes that there is still no real agreement about whether "borderline" is a clear-cut diagnostic entity. Two major perspectives in psychoanalysis are those of Knight (1953a) and Kernberg (1973). According to Knight (1953a) "borderline states" are positions or way stations in the process of decompensation from a nonpsychotic to a psychotic state, or in the process of regression from a neurotic to a psychotic level of psychic organization. The term might be used to describe a patient who does not appear neurotic but is not schizophrenic (Moore & Fine, 1990).

"Borderline personality organization" as defined by Kernberg (1973) refers to a character structure that shows (1) essentially intact reality testing; (2) contradictory early identifications leading to a lack of an integrated ego identity; (3) a predominance of splitting; and (4) separation problems.

One of the major difficulties in treating borderline patients—who are like narcissistic children—is that they demand immediate gratification and prefer action over verbalization, reflection, and understanding (Moore & Fine, 1990).

Sexual Problems

One of psychoanalysis's major contributions to the mental health professions as well as to the public at large is its sensitive, humane, and comprehensive approach to sexuality. Psychoanalytically oriented practitioners and theorists view sexuality as an interpersonal experience between two human beings who bring their history, egos, ids, superegos, childhood fantasies, memories, defenses, and much more to the sexual encounter.

To the psychoanalytically oriented practitioner, the patient's overt sexual behavior is much less crucial than how he or she experiences himself or herself and the partner while engaging in sex. Sex to the psychoanalytically oriented is much more than a bodily experience; it is an emotional transaction in which the individuals reveal deep feelings about their body images, self-images, self-esteem, and their capacity for intimacy and empathy to each other—their complete metapsychologies are at work (Fine, 1982; Freud, 1905; Strean, 1979).

It should come as no surprise that those who cannot easily trust others are not going to enjoy the intimacy inherent in a sexual relationship. The tenderness, movements, and closeness in sex recapitulate all of psychosexual development. For example, if a couple has problems with trust (orality), it will appear in their sexual relationship.

> Sarah and Joe Dillon, a couple in their thirties married two years, sought therapeutic help because neither of them could enjoy their sexual relationship. Both frequently experienced nausea, depression, and anxiety when they just thought about having sex with each other.
> As their life stories unfolded and their feelings and fantasies were discussed in treatment, it became clear that the Dillons had many unresolved infantile wishes that frightened them. Each wanted to be an infant in sex but resented being in what felt like a very vulnerable position with the other. Each ascribed parental qualities to the partner and hated each other for their "controlling, dominant" attitudes. In effect, each of the Dillons felt weak and helpless (like babies) in sex. By avoiding sex, they avoided confronting their unresolved orality and infantile fantasies.

Patients who have sexual difficulties often experience sex as an anal experience—"dirty," "putting out," and "submitting." Similar to children who refuse to defecate or urinate "for" their parents, many adults see nothing in sex for themselves—only for their partners who they unconsciously make arbitrary and demanding parents.

Many husbands and wives have a tendency to turn their spouses into parental figures and then feel sex is a form of forbidden incest. These individuals frequently find themselves sexually inhibited and/or can find pleasure in sex only with an extramarital partner (Strean, 1980).

Impotence in men

The impotent man often equates his sexual partner with his mother and wants to compete aggressively with his father. The incestuous fantasies that are recapitulated with his sexual partner and the murderous thoughts that he unconsciously entertains toward a father-figure arouse much anxiety. To ward off his conflicts and anxiety, he does not allow himself to have sexual pleasure (Fenichel, 1945).

Sexual displeasure in women

The woman who inhibits herself sexually may also be equating her sexual partner with the parent of the opposite sex and then punishes herself for her rivalry with her mother (Fenichel, 1945).

Usually sexual inhibitions in both women and men are overdetermined—they have more than one cause. For example, women who have unresolved oedipal problems often regress and begin to identify with members of the opposite sex. Then the homosexual fantasies they experience cause further anxiety and so they avoid sex even more. Hence, the patient's forbidden oral, anal, and phallic oedipal conflicts may all be operative in his or her sexual inhibitions, making sexual problems difficult to resolve and often needing prolonged psychotherapy. Usually such individuals who become lovers or spouses end up with partners who have similar psychosexual conflicts. Consequently each tends to reinforce the other's sexual inhibitions.

Homosexuality

Few subjects within and outside psychoanalysis have aroused as much controversy as homosexuality. For many years most psychoanalysts tended to view homosexuality as a sign of arrested development, a regression from the oedipal conflict (Fenichel, 1945), and/or a fixation at an earlier preoedipal period (Socarides, 1978). In effect, although psychoanalysts did not discount constitutional, hormonal, or other innate predispositions, the majority of them saw homosexuality as emerging from hostile family atmospheres in which parents did not provide appropriate role models for their offspring (Fine, 1982).

Influenced in part by the political climate and the civil rights movement, many psychoanalysts have shifted their views about homosexuality—seeing it less a function of faulty psychosexual development and more as a biological given. In *Being Homosexual: Gay Men and Their Development*, Richard Isay (1989), a psychoanalyst, presents his conviction that sexual orientation, whether it be homosexual, heterosexual, or bisexual, "is constitutionally set and immutable from birth" (p. 21). Furthermore, he has found no differences in the parenting of gay men as compared to heterosexual men. Therefore, he concludes that a genetic factor is responsible for sexual orientation.

Arguing for a more neutral attitude toward homosexuality and not seeing it as a sexual perversion, another psychoanalyst, Richard Friedman (1988) in *Male Homosexuality: A Contemporary Psychoanalytic Perspective*, feels that psychoanalysts have been too rigid in their diagnostic appraisals of homosexual patients. States Friedman:

> There is no homosexual or heterosexual character type. In fact, it would appear that homosexuality, bisexuality, and heterosexuality are distributed across the entire range of character

types and character structures. (p. 81)

Psychoanalysts, at this time, have very different points of view about homosexuality. There are many analysts who are unconvinced by presentations of a constitutional basis for homosexuality. These analysts, for example Socarides (1978) and Fine (1982), still view human sexuality as a consequence of psychological development and not physiological happenstance. Further clinical experience and research will be necessary to resolve these disparate points of view.

What makes the heat that surrounds the subject of homosexuality difficult to reduce, and replace with light instead, is that homosexuality means many different things to many different people. For some, it is a life-style; for others, it is a civil rights issue; and for still others, it is a psychological problem. Homosexuality arouses anxiety for many individuals, causing discussion to be more defensive and argumentative than enlightening and informative (Strean, 1984).

Perversions

Like the more generic term "sexual deviant," the term "perversion" has had pejorative connotations frequently. Consequently, those patients suffering from problems such as fetishism or exhibitionism have not always received the understanding they deserve.

From a psychoanalytic point of view, all perversions are sexual substitutes. The fetishist, the exhibitionist, or the sadist are individuals who are terrified of adult sexuality and therefore they regress to sexual behavior that is more appropriate for children. Although their guilt feelings may oppose their impulses, they feel compelled to give in to their wishes in the hope of achieving some positive pleasure (Fenichel, 1945).

Eric, a man in his 30s, after several months of therapy, confessed to his therapist that he had a constant "compulsion" to exhibit his penis to women. He did this at work, in libraries, in the movies, and elsewhere. He knew "it wasn't the right thing to do," but he could not help himself.

As Eric felt safe enough to discuss his exhibitionism in more depth, he talked a great deal in therapy about his fear of male authorities and then went on to reveal his strong yearning to be close to a father-figure. It became quite clear that to defend against his forbidden homosexual desires and wish to be "Daddy's little girl," Eric was compulsively saying, "See, I'm not a girl. I'm a man. I have a penis."

If we recognize that all perversions are sexual substitutes because the patient is extremely frightened of an interpersonal relationship, the perversion begins to make sense. Fetishism is an attempt to avoid human contact because such contact is more dangerous than touching underwear. Sadism is an attempt to avoid feeling vulnerable in the human sexual contact, and masochism is a means to avoid experiencing sadism in sex. Every perversion is a protection against a fantasied danger (Strean, 1983).

The Psychoneuroses

The major factors that contribute to a psychoneurosis have already been discussed earlier in this chapter. To recapitulate briefly, the patient has sexual and aggressive wishes that are unacceptable and therefore create anxiety. Defenses are utilized to protect the patient against anxiety but they are not strong enough to bind the anxiety. As a result, symptoms such as obsessions, compulsions, and phobias erupt. A symptom is a "compromise formation" expressing in disguised form a patient's unacceptable sexual and aggressive impulses as well as his or her anxiety. There are three major psychoneuroses: obsessive-compulsive neurosis, anxiety hysteria, and conversion hysteria (Brenner, 1955).

The *obsessive-compulsive* neurotic is tormented by continuous and unwanted "foreign" thoughts and/or feels compelled to perform certain actions over which he or she has little control. The patient is in a constant struggle between strong impulses, usually sadistic, to hurt others and an equally strong desire to punish himself or herself for "evil" impulses. The compulsion or obsession is a compromise between two opposing forces: the id's wish to aggress and the superego's wish for punishment. The ego compromises by forming the obsessive or compulsive symptom.

Several forms of obsessions and compulsions are well known. The person with a hand-washing compulsion must continually clean away dirty thoughts; the housewife who must constantly check the gas jets is attempting to cope with wishes to burn down the house; the parishioner in church who has obsessive thoughts to defame God is feeling furious about being in church and praying but is very guilty about these sadistic wishes.

The conflicts in obsessive-compulsive neurosis invariably deal with struggles between love and hate, cleanliness and dirt, right and wrong. One of the paramount features of this neurosis is that patients suffering from it believe their thoughts can kill; they view their thoughts as omnipotent and magical, that is, to think, for example of murder or incest, is to do it (Cameron, 1963).

The patient suffering from *anxiety hysteria* is characterized by pervasive anxiety. Most of the time the anxiety is attached to special objects or situations and expresses itself in the form of phobias, for example, strong fears of the dark, animals, foods, airplanes, cars, and other "dangerous" objects. The dreaded object that must be avoided usually symbolizes sexually exciting situations. For example, darkness can arouse forbidden sexual fantasies which create anxiety. To diminish the anxiety, the person avoids dark rooms.

> Florence was a 19-year-old college student who sought treatment because she was terrified of being in elevators. She became extremely anxious in elevators, trembled, and often vomited. She spent hours going up and down stairs to avoid facing the dread of being in an elevator.
>
> In treatment Florence learned that "going up" and "coming down" was, to her, reminiscent of strong sexual fantasies that were frightening and unacceptable to her. The more she could verbalize in treatment her sexual fantasies, particularly incestuous ones toward an older brother, the less phobic she became.

Hysterical patients often suffer from much guilt because of strong but forbidden incestuous and murderous desires, that is, oedipal wishes. Frequently they believe they are going to be punished by abandonment, loss of love, death, or mutilation. They also tend to dramatize their emotions—an exhibitionistic trait appropriate to the excitement associated with this neurosis. Fearful of losing love, they are eager to please others (Cameron, 1963; Fenichel, 1945).

In *conversion hysteria* the patient's dynamics are similar to those of an anxiety hysteric except that the symptoms are expressed in a physical form. The physical symptoms give expression to instinctual impulses that previously had been repressed, and the organ of the body that is chosen expresses the patient's conflict.

> George, an army recruit, was referred to a mental hygiene clinic on post because no physi-

cal component was observed when both of his legs were paralyzed. Intensive psychotherapy was initiated. George revealed strong wishes to kick his superiors and strong reluctance to march and wait on lines. These sadistic and rebellious wishes conflicted with severe superego prohibitions which created intense anxiety. George coped with his anxiety by developing paralytic symptoms.

Addictions

Sufferers from addictions are trying to satisfy a strong emotional hunger which they do not feel comfortable in securing from another human being. Just as perversions are sexual substitutes, addictions to food, tobacco, and drugs are all substitutes for interpersonal gratification. In his recent monograph, *Psychoanalytic Approaches to Addiction*, Angelo Smaldino (1991) and his colleagues demonstrate how the addictive personality forms "a transference" to the food, drug, or tobacco and these items are to the patient the equivalent of a person. In a paper "Observations on Countertransference, Addiction, and Treatability," Mitchell May (1991) states:

> Relationships have unconscious wishes attached to them, which are used for defense and are need gratifying; often they serve the repetition compulsion. The relationship between a patient and a substance has all of these ingredients attached to it. There is a transference to the substance. It may be a relationship with a nonperson, but it is a relationship just the same. (p. 2)

Inasmuch as addictive personalities frequently feel distrustful of people, they resort to the solitary pleasure of the addiction. Taking a needle or food or a cigarette is like feeding oneself. The addictive personality would rather do this than depend on someone else for pleasure.

Usually substance abusers and other sufferers from addictions have strong omnipotent fantasies. When they are on "a high" they feel they can control the world (Smaldino, 1991). Berthelsdorf (1976), in his psychoanalytic work on addictions, comments on the patient's strong passive wishes and conviction of his or her own weakness. Imbibing drugs, for example, can compensate for feelings of weakness and emptiness. Berthelsdorf (1976) also notes how very resentful these patients are and how addictive behavior is frequently an expression of defiance.

Psychosomatic Problems

Most people are aware of physiological accompaniments to various emotions. If we are angry, we may find ourselves breathing quickly, perspiring, and trembling. Loving feelings are often accompanied by fast heartbeats and other visceral sensations.

Even to the casual observer it is apparent that undischarged quantities of anger can lead to a migraine headache or insomnia; unfulfilled dependency wishes that are unacceptable and cause anxiety can bring on an ulcer; and frustrated libidinal yearnings can induce heart conditions. Expressions such as "That was a heartbreaker," "He gives me a headache," "I could not stomach her (him)" demonstrate how the mind and body are intimately connected. There is some controversy about the unconscious meaning of psychosomatic illnesses. Some writers contend that they are expressions of dammed up excitation and tension and do not express a unique set of dynamic conflicts (Glover, 1949). Others allege that a part of the body is unconsciously selected to express a unique conflict (Fenichel, 1945). In the second view an ulcer might express undischarged and conflicted dependency feelings; colitis might mask a wish to withhold defiant anal sadistic fantasies; and enuresis might disguise feelings of "being pissed off."

> George Hill, a 26-year-old bachelor, would develop acute migraine headaches every time he visited his widowed mother. The headaches were so intense, he would not be able to function. After vomiting and "sleeping off" his headache, he would go home, relieved, only to have an ulcer attack in a day or two.
>
> The migraine headaches were an expression of George's rage. He felt compelled to take care of his mother but resented it. His resentment induced anxiety; consequently, he repressed it. However, anything repressed shows up somewhere. For George, his rage emerged in the headaches.
>
> However, when George separated from his mother, although he was unaware of it, he missed her. His acute dependency feelings, which also induced anxiety and were repressed, manifested themselves in his ulcer attacks.
>
> When George could talk in therapy about his unacceptable dependency fantasies and aggressive thoughts, his psychosomatic problems diminished.

Character Disorders

In contrast to the individual with symptomatic neuroses, the one with a character disorder does not have *ego-alien* symptoms such as a phobia, obsession, or compulsion; this person has *ego-syntonic* character traits that feel like "the right way" to cope. Character traits such as stinginess, demandingness, or promiscuity, are indicative of conflict, but the person does not suffer from them; he or she may induce suffering in others with his or her rigidity. The following are some examples of character disorders.

The *oral character* is the person who is perenially seeking symbiotic mergers with almost everyone in his or her social orbit. People with oral character disorders are demanding individuals who, like infants, want instant gratification. If they do not get what they want, they are very insistent and keep trying. This very narcissistic individual knows little autonomy and like the baby, he or she talks (babbles) incessantly, demands constant approbation, and must feel attached to another person in order to feel some identity (English & Pearson, 1945; Fenichel, 1945; Strean, 1979).

The *anal character*, an individual whose instinctual life is anally oriented, was discussed by Freud in *The New Introductory Lectures* (1933). He or she has certain dominant character traits which are essentially reaction formations against anal erotic desires. The main traits are orderliness, frugality, and obstinancy. These ego syntonic character traits express concomitantly a resistance against messiness and sloppiness as well as an obedience to the demands of a punitive superego. The anal character is one who would love "to shit all over the place" and yet is so scared of these wishes that he or she maintains unusual care around cleanliness and orderliness.

Individuals with *hysterical characters* are usually very passionate and sanguine and very often are quite aggrandizing in their interpersonal relationships. Often they are quite infantile as they express themselves emotionally and on occasion are subject to illusions. Their character traits express a conflict between strong but repressed sexual strivings and strong fears of sexual wishes, often of an oedipal nature. The hysterical character tends to sexualize most relations and is often inclined towards suggestibility, emotional outbreaks, chaotic behavior, and histrionics (English & Pearson, 1945; Fenichel, 1945).

The *psychopath* is usually impulsive, extremely narcissistic, and unwilling to curb aggressive and sexual impulses because he or she does not feel any obligation to cooperate with what appears to be an uncooperative world (Cameron, 1963). Often this individual has a very punitive superego, which he or she rebels against. Criminal and other antisocial behavior may often be seen in individuals who have a conscience but cannot tolerate its voices. Their rebellion is really against the superego's inner voices (Glover, 1960).

The *paranoid character* is usually quite fearful of hidden persecutors, people toward whom he or she feels an unconscious attraction, often homosexual. The attraction creates enormous anxiety and therefore is projected onto another person. The other person, that is, the persecutor, is often accused of improper sexual motives. Frequently the paranoid character is a guilt-ridden person who often anticipates punishment. Hating themselves and feeling very ashamed of their sexual and aggressive fantasies, paranoid characters seem very ready for assaults from their environments, which they experience as omnipotent and punishing (Reich, 1948).

In completing our survey of clinical diagnoses, it is important to reemphasize that diagnostic labels have many limitations. They do not usually give us a deep understanding of the patient's unique psychic structure or dynamics. They often serve to stigmatize and stereotype the patient. This hinders the process of individualizing the diagnostic assessment of the patient and can interfere with treatment planning and the treatment process.

RECOMMENDED READINGS

For a comprehensive review of the major neuroses, psychoses, and character problems from a psychoanalytic point of view, Fenichel's *Psychoanalytic Theory of Neuroses* is excellent. A full explication in very clear language of the unconscious processes in mental conflict is Brenner's *An Elementary Textbook of Psychoanalysis*. In language written for the layman, English and Pearson's *Emotional Problems of Living* discusses psychopathology in children and adults.

To be up-to-date on all the research, treatment, and diagnostic problems on the borderline patient, see Fine's *Current and Historical Perspectives on the Borderline Patient*. The most humane and sensitive treatment on the diagnosis and therapy of the schizophrenic patient from a psychoanalytic perspective is Karon and Vandenbos's *Psychotherapy of Schizophrenia: The Treatment of Choice*. For a detailed description of the intensive analytic treatment of a schizophrenic patient, *The Severed Soul*, by Strean and Freeman may be of interest.

One of the most up-to-date books on the psychoanalytic treatment of addictions is Smaldino's *Psychoanalytic Approaches to Addiction*. See also Berthelsdorf's "Survey of the Successful Analysis of a Young Man Addicted to Heroin."

For good psychoanalytic definitions of neuroses and psychoses and other clinical entities, see *Psychoanalytic Terms and Concepts* by Moore and Fine. Also, Cameron's *Personality Development and Psychopathology* is clear and helpful.

A clear discussion of gender problems from a psychoanalytic perspective is Kissen's *Gender and Psychoanalytic Treatment*. For a review of sexual dysfunctions and their psychoanalytic treatment see Strean's *The Sexual Dimension*.

4

A PSYCHOANALYTIC
VIEW OF
PSYCHOTHERAPY

Just as the psychoanalytic theory of human behavior contends that the individual's adaptation to life cannot be fully understood unless id wishes, ego defenses, superego prohibitions, and history are exposed, so, too, a patient cannot be substantially helped unless he or she becomes more aware of wishes, defenses, and superego admonitions and recognizes how past relationships and experiences are being recapitulated in the present. Psychoanalysis alleges that if symptoms are to be given up, character problems diminished, and psychosomatic ills lessened, the patient must become sensitized to how he or she *unconsciously* arranges a good part of his or her maladaptive script.

As stated in the Preface, it is the thesis of this book that all therapists can profit from assimilating certain psychoanalytic principles into their therapeutic repertoires. In this chapter we will review and discuss the major therapeutic concepts utilized by mainstream psychoanalysts and in doing so will emphasize those principles that are applicable to most therapeutic situations, regardless of the clinician's theoretical predilections or clinical preferences.

THE FUNDAMENTAL RULE: FREE ASSOCIATION

To help the patient become more sensitized to how he or she writes a maladaptive script, the patient is encouraged to say *everything* that comes to mind—feelings, thoughts, memories, fantasies, dreams, and whatever else emerges. Although no patient in any setting (even on a couch in a formal analysis 5 times a week) fully tells the whole truth and nothing but the truth, the fundamental rule is an ideal that patients are asked to *try* to follow.

Even though all patients resist obeying the fundamental rule in their own unique ways (we shall discuss the universality of resistance later in this chapter), there are several rationales for the institution of the fundamental rule (Freud, 1904).

As patients permit themselves to say what is on their minds about what is troubling them, by listening to their associations that were been previously defended against, patients learn new things about themselves. For example, as a husband associates to his anger and fear of his wife, he will eventually see and hear how he is making his wife a punitive mother. As a mother freely associates to her stresses in her relationship with her daughter, she may see how she is projecting part of her past onto her daughter and perceiving the daughter as if she was a part of her debased self-image.

If the therapist neither praises nor condemns while the patient freely associates, the patient slowly begins to feel like a prisoner who has been set free. Like the well-understood child who is not berated for what has been confessed, most patients soon after they begin to free associate start to like themselves more as they interact with a therapist who appears to be a benign superego.

Usually when patients free associate, they begin to recall memories that influence their current functioning. They begin to see how a fight with a friend may be part of an unresolved conflict with a sibling, or a fear of a boss might be a continuation of an old ambivalent relationship with a parent.

As the patient is given the opportunity to say everything to a neutral listener, the patient begins to have feelings toward the therapist. These *transference reactions*—which we discuss in detail later in this chapter—when examined, help the patient gain a better understanding of how he or she distorts interpersonal relationships. For example, a male patient afraid of women may assume that his female therapist is repudiating his associations, as his mother contradicted him in the past. Understanding transference responses, which is one of the unique features of psychoanalytically oriented therapy, helps patients see reality more clearly.

Through free association, patients begin to realize some of the factors that account for their behavior and appreciate that to go on condemning themselves for their fears and wishes is counterproductive. Very often this nonjudgmental attitude is transferred to family or friends. As patients appreciate themselves more, they start to appreciate others more. In turn, friends and family begin to appreciate the patient more.

If the patient is going to free associate and eventually becomes aware of the unconscious meaning of thoughts, feelings, fantasies, and memories, the therapist must demonstrate his or her confidence in the patient's capacity to communicate and derive meaning from the associations. For the patient to develop more confidence, he or she must learn first to enjoy his or her mental contents, that is, the free associations. This can take place only if the therapist firmly believes in the value and utility of the fundamental rule (Strean, 1979).

RESISTANCE

Initially most patients welcome the idea of saying everything that comes into their minds and usually feel better as a result. However, sooner or later the therapy becomes painful and creates anxiety. As patients discover parts of themselves that have been hidden from them, as they confront sexual and aggressive fantasies, and recover embarrassing memories, they begin to feel guilt and shame. To protect themselves against the uncomfortable feelings of guilt and shame and to ward off the anxiety that produces it, patients will stop producing material and cease examining themselves. When that happens we refer to this behavior as *resistance*.

Resistance is any action or attitude of the patient's that impedes the course of therapeutic work. Inasmuch as every patient, to some extent, wants unconsciously to preserve the status quo, all therapy must be carried on in the face of some resistance (Strean, 1990).

What are referred to as defenses in the patient's daily life, for example projection, denial, and repression, emerge as resistances in treatment.

> Joe Zanger sought therapy because he was not "turned on" by his wife. He spent most of his sessions talking about how his wife was "full of hostility." Later in the treatment he talked a great deal about his boss's and colleagues "sadism." Still later, he complained to the therapist that the latter was "always showing contempt."
>
> In his daily life, Joe projected his anger onto everyone else and denied his own. In his treat-

ment he filled many therapy hours avoiding an examination of his anger and projecting it onto everyone else, including the therapist.

It is important to keep in mind that resistance is not created by the therapy. The therapeutic situation activates anxiety, and the patient then uses habitual defense mechanisms to oppose the therapist and the therapy (Fine, 1982; Strean, 1990). To a greater or lesser degree, resistances are present from the first session to the last.

Psychoanalytically oriented therapy attempts to uncover how patients resist, what they are resisting, and why they are doing so. The purpose of a resistance is to avoid a danger. The patient may be afraid of being abandoned because of certain wishes, unloved for certain activities, demeaned for certain values, or isolated for certain behavior. In contrast to other therapies that evade resistances or attempt to overcome them by praise, punishment, drugs, shock, suggestion, or persuasion, psychoanalytically oriented psychotherapy seeks to uncover the cause, purpose, mode, and history of resistances (Greenson, 1967).

Various attempts have been made by psychoanalysts to classify resistances. The first attempt was in Freud's (1926) *Inhibitions, Symptoms, and Anxiety.*

1. When using *repression* or other defenses like *projection* or *denial*, the patient uses habitual defenses in the treatment to ward off the eruption of sexual and aggressive fantasies because they present a danger.
2. In *transference resistances*, the patient perceives the therapist as if he or she were a figure of the past. Instead of facing unpleasant memories and feelings from the past, the patient ascribes parental qualities to the therapist and then feels the therapist is rejecting, provocative, seductive—or any other characteristic

reminiscent of a parent or parental figure.

3. In *epinosic gain*, the patient strives to maintain the gratifications and protections that the neurosis (or other maladaptation) provides.

4. When there is *superego resistance*, the patient berates himself or herself with guilt and self-punishment because of unacceptable wishes, behavior, or fantasies. This is sometimes referred to as the "negative therapeutic reaction" (Freud, 1923).

5. With *id resistance*, by continuing to seek gratification of unrealistic childish wishes, the patient persists in trying to be an omnipotent infant and have all of his or her demands met immediately.

Commenting on resolving resistances, Freud (1914a) stated:

> The working through of the resistances may, in practice, turn out to be an arduous task for the subject of the analysis and a trial of patience for the analyst. Nevertheless, it is a part of the work which effects the greatest changes in a patient and which distinguishes analytic treatment from any [other] kind of treatment. (p. 145)

In 1955 Edward Glover distinguished between "gross" and "unobtrusive" resistances. Gross resistances refer to obvious behaviors such as consistent lateness for sessions, refusal to talk, or refusal to pay fees. Unobtrusive resistances refer to behaviors of which the patient is unaware, such as excessive compliance, psychosomatic ailments, or forgetting appointments. Greenson (1967) classified resistances according to their sources (id, ego, superego); their fixation points (oral, anal, phallic-oedipal, latency, adolescent); the types of defenses used (for example, repression, denial); the clinical diagnosis (for example, anxiety hysteria, borderline personality); and finally, whether a resistance is ego-alien or ego-syntonic. Fine (1982) divides resistances into those involving refusal to comply with basic requests, for example, lateness, refusal to pay, refusal to talk, and those of a more subtle nature, such as an overemphasis on reality, unreasonable demands, and the negative therapeutic reaction.

Examples of Resistance

In any discussion of resistances, it is important to emphasize that the specific behavior, such as lateness to an appointment or refusal to pay a fee, does not tell us very much until we hear more about it from the patient. The lateness can express everything from defiance to a fear of intimacy. Sometimes the one act can express more than one motive.

Lateness

> Barbara Young, a 24-year-old single woman, came for therapy because she was unsuccessful in sustaining relationships with men. After falling madly in love with them, she would abruptly break up with her boyfriends.
>
> After 3 months of twice a week treatment with a male therapist, Barbara began coming late for interviews. When this was explored in the treatment, Barbara at first denied that her lateness had any meaning. After awhile she was able to tell her male therapist that she didn't want him to feel "too important" or "too cocky" at her expense.
>
> Barbara's lateness was a manifestation of her competition with men. As she learned that her competition was related to envious feelings of

her younger brother, her lateness diminished
and her relationships with male friends improved.

Very often a resistive piece of behavior is an attempt to
place the therapist in the same hated position in which the
patient was placed in childhood.

> Charlie Wolfe, a man in his 40s who came into
> treatment because of constant arguments with
> bosses, began to arrive late for his therapy in the
> third month of treatment.   As the issue was
> explored, Charlie was able to acknowledge "some
> secret pleasure" in keeping his therapist waiting
> for him.   Further discussion revealed that this
> was an attempt at revenge inasmuch as his mother
> used to keep Charlie waiting for her for hours and
> always offered spurious reasons when she was
> asked about it.

Silence

Just as lateness can have many meanings, so does a patient's
silence. Silence can be an expression of love such as is
experienced by lovers after sex. It can also be an accompaniment of symbiotic merger or can express defiance. As
with any resistance, silence can be overdetermined.

> Shirley Victor was a recently married woman
> of 21. She came into therapy because she was
> completely unable to participate in sex. She would
> become very sullen, break out in hives, and often
> vomited when her husband attempted to have sex
> with her.
> In her therapy with a male clinician, she was
> silent, often for complete sessions. When the
> therapist did not force her to talk, she was able to
> relax eventually. After about 6 months of almost
> complete silence in treatment, Shirley was able

to find many reasons to account for her silences. Talking was like "putting out sexually" and she deeply resented it. It reminded her of working hard for her parents and not being appreciated. Shirley had strong fantasies "to just do nothing" and being silent in treatment was her way to gratify this wish.

Reluctance to pay fees

Usually a reluctance to pay fees expresses some resentment about the therapy and the therapist. Inasmuch as fees are one of the few things that therapists can demand of patients, they may try to hurt the therapist by withholding what is wanted. Many patients want to be indulged as children and therefore the idea of paying a fee to a parental figure seems ludicrous.

Sam Ungar, 17 years old, had been much indulged by his parents. When his therapist thought it would be a good idea for Sam to bring the monthly fee to the therapist, he protested vehemently. He bellowed, "You are supposed to take care of me. I'm not supposed to take care of you." His strong id resistance was present for many months in the therapy; it took much time to resolve.

Overemphasis on the present

Most patients, much of the time, like to believe they are victims of other people's unresolved problems. Husbands blame wives for their interpersonal problems and vice versa; parents blame children for their mutual problems and vice versa; patients blame therapists and vice versa, and so on. It is difficult for most individuals to take responsibility for their intrapsychic and interpersonal

problems. They do not want to see how they are recapitu-
lating their childhood in the present. Consequently, some
patients will come to their therapy sessions and talk
exclusively about an unresolved reality problem in their
daily lives that seems overwhelming, failing to see that
their preoccupation is a resistance.

> Max Thompson, a married man in his 50s, went
> into treatment because of sexual impotence. How-
> ever, he spent all of his time during sessions
> talking about his lack of money. He had dis-
> placed his feelings of sexual inadequacy onto his
> financial problems. It took his therapist many
> months before he could help Max accept the idea
> that he should take a look at the history of his
> anxiety in his sexual relationship with his wife.

Overemphasis on the past

When the patient's past has been painful and embarrassing, to avoid shameful memories and recalling difficult
traumas, the patient may focus exclusively on present
circumstances. On the other hand, when patients overem-
phasize their past, they are usually frightened to reveal
and examine some current issues.

> Mary Roberts, a single woman in her early 30s,
> sought therapy because she wanted to be married
> but kept having a series of unfulfilling love affairs
> instead. In her treatment she focused exclusively
> on her childhood and talked a great deal about
> her father. When her therapist became aware of
> Mary's resistance and wondered if there was
> something in the present that was difficult to talk
> about, Mary became very withdrawn. It turned
> out that rather than discuss a current affair she
> was having with a married man, Mary talked in
> therapy about her childhood relationship with

her father—not realizing that this was what she was acting out symbolically with her married lover.

There are many forms of resistance, other than the ones we have just reviewed. As we have emphasized, resistances may be overt or covert, direct or indirect, unobtrusive or gross. Whatever form resistance takes, it is important for practitioners to keep in mind that resistances are present from the first phone call to the last session. All patients, no matter how much they want their lives to be different, fear change. All patients want to avoid the dangers and anxieties that self-exposure entails. That is why resistances are essential facts of therapeutic life, and understanding the reasons for their unique expression is essential for all patients and therapists. This is particularly true of the most ubiquitous resistance, transference.

TRANSFERENCE

Although Freud and many of his followers separated transference and resistance as two distinct phenomena, transference must be viewed as a resistance because it preserves the status quo and protects the patient against real or fantasied danger.

Freud (1912) singled out the notion of transference for much discussion. He pointed out that it is a universal phenomenon that dominates each individual's interpersonal relationships. Transference exists in all relationships, psychoanalysis alleges. Because all of us bring our unique histories, ego functioning, superego mandates, fantasies, and fears into all relationships, nobody perceives anybody without some distortion. In all interpersonal relationships nonrational, subjective factors are present.

Freud's notions on transference (1912, 1914a, 1926)

have had a strong impact on therapists of many different theoretical perspectives. Freud pointed out that if clinicians do not understand how they are being experienced by their patients, they cannot be very helpful to them. All patients respond to their therapists' interventions (verbal and nonverbal) in terms of their transferences. If a patient loves the therapist, the patient will be inclined to accept most of the therapist's interventions. If the patient hates the therapist, even the most neutral question by the therapist will be suspect. Finally, if the patient has mixed feelings toward the therapist, almost all of the therapist's comments and actions will be experienced ambivalently.

One of the major contributions of psychoanalysis to psychotherapy has been to demonstrate that all patients— regardless of the setting in which they are being treated, of the therapeutic modality, or the therapist's skills and years of experience—will respond to interventions in terms of the transference. It is important for clinicians of all persuasions to recognize that the most brilliant statement in the world by a therapist will be refuted by a patient who is in a negative transference. It is equally important for clinicians to recognize that the most inaccurate statement in the world will be positively accepted if the patient is in a postive transference.

A major task of every therapist, psychoanalysis asserts (Freud, 1914a), is to help patients see how and why they experience the therapist the way they do. Why does one patient argue with the therapist almost every time the latter says something? Why does another patient act like a compliant child and accept almost everything the therapist says?

Although transference reactions are always traceable to childhood, there is not always a simple one-to-one correspondence between the past and present. Frequently there can be a "compensatory fantasy" (Fine, 1982) to make up for what was lacking in childhood. In effect, the patient fantasizes that the therapist is somebody that a parent should have been.

Freud (1905, 1912, 1914a, 1926) and other psychoanalysts have discovered that transference reactions can take many forms. The patient can proclaim loving feelings toward the therapist, but dreams, fantasies, and other resistances (for example, forgetting an appointment, bouncing a check) may reveal the opposite. Similarly, statements of hatred may defend against warm feelings.

A very common use of the transference is the patient's projection onto the therapist of the patient's psychic structure—id wishes, ego defenses, or superego mandates. Many therapists are perceived as dirty old men and women because the patient projects his or her own id wishes onto the therapist. An even more frequent phenomenon is the patient projecting onto the therapist his or her own superego mandates. This is why patients are frequently anticipating criticism or other forms of punishment from the therapist.

As therapist and patient accept transference as a fact of therapeutic life and consistently examine the patient's transference responses, they gain an appreciation of the nature of the patient's conflicts and those aspects of the patient's history that are contributing to his or her dysfunctional behavior (Strean, 1990).

Examples of Transference

Idealizing the therapist

Most individuals yearn for a perfect parent. In therapy, where the patient often for the first time in his or life finds an empathetic listener who asks for little but gives a great deal, it is easy for the patient to believe, "At last, I have found the ideal parent." Then the patient soaks in every word of the therapist, truly believes that Paradise has been rediscovered, and feels like an overjoyed child.

If the therapist does not recognize that he or she is being severely distorted, the client will be hurt! When the patient's childish admiration of the therapist is not viewed as a resistance, then the patient will never achieve much autonomy, self-confidence, or self-esteem. He or she will remain a psychological child tied to a parent.

> Saul Quirk, a man in his 40s, sought treatment for a depression. Almost as soon as he began therapy, he felt much better and his depression lifted. He felt that his female therapist was "the most nurturing, kindest, attentive woman" he had ever met in his life. The therapist enjoyed Saul's laudatory comments, and rather than help him see that he was defending himself against being a potent male by acting like a compliant, admiring child, she soaked in Saul's adoring comments.
>
> When it became apparent to the therapist and later to Saul himself that he was not growing from his therapeutic experience, the therapist began to monitor her exultation when Saul complimented her. Eventually Saul got in touch with the aggression behind his childish facade and began to see how frightened he was to assert himself—a major factor in his depression.

The negative therapeutic reaction

As Freud worked with more patients, he began to observe a frequent phenomenon. He noted that many patients who could achieve insight into their problems and accept his interpretations did not improve. Freud (1923) concluded that there was an inner force at work that prevented patients from utilizing their insights. He identified this force as a superego resistance.

Freud and the many mental health professionals who have followed him have learned that there are many patients who cannot tolerate the idea of feeling better and enjoying a productive life. Almost every time they do feel some pleasure, they feel guilty about it. What clinicians since Freud have been able to appreciate is that guilt-ridden patients with punitive superegos are ones who have strong hostile wishes. When these patients succeed at anything, they worry about whom they have destroyed.

The patient who has a punitive superego and therefore is harboring strong hostile fantasies, brings this self-destructive modus vivendi to the therapeutic situation, like all patients would. When such an individual enters therapy, does not improve, and points out that he or she won't ever get better, this individual is directing anger toward the therapist and is unconsciously trying to defeat the therapeutic process.

> Katherine Patterson, a single woman in her late 30s, entered therapy because her "whole life was a mess." She was "unsuccessful" in her job as a teacher, was "a social misfit" with men, argued with her female friends, was often depressed, and occasionally suicidal.
>
> Although Katherine absorbed her male therapist's interpretations—even acknowledging her negative transference reactions and seeing that they were related to her strong death wishes toward both parents and a brother—she would always return to her misery after a few days of relaxation.
>
> Inasmuch as she eventually had to defeat almost everything the therapist said, Katherine had to defeat the notion that she was trying to defeat the therapist at every turn. Eventually she left therapy, feeling that it had not helped her very much.

Although most patients with a negative therapeutic reaction eventually become aware of the futility of their battles with the therapist, there are some like Katherine Patterson who derive more satisfaction from fighting than cooperating. They are the patients who go from one therapist to another trying to get help but unconsciously work hard to defeat the process.

The erotic transference

Accompanying the positive transference are usually childish sexual fantasies. When patients have found the "ideal" person in the form of a therapist, they fall in love with him or her and want to have an affair.

As we have pointed out repeatedly, a piece of behavior by itself tells us little. Therefore, the erotic transference has to be studied carefully before the practitioner can infer its meaning and offer explanations to the patient about it. As Reuben Fine (1982) has said in *The Healing of the Mind*,

> The erotic transference may, like any other libidinal manifestation, have almost any dynamic meaning. It may be a bid for reassurance, a cover-up for hostility, an expression of envy, an oral-incorporative wish, a defense against homosexuality, or all of these at different times.... It is not possible to tell in advance what meaning erotic feelings may have or even to equate different patients merely because they display similar behavior. Each person has to be understood in terms of his or her own background and life experience. (p. 95)

One often overlooked dimension of the erotic transference is that the patient is trying to remove the therapist from his or her therapeutic position. That is why the erotic transference is always a resistance to treatment, and accompanying it are usually unconscious hostile fantasies toward the therapist.

> Sally Olsen, a married woman in her mid-30s, sought therapy because she was very dissatisfied with her marriage. She derived limited emotional and sexual satisfaction from her relationship with her husband and was seriously thinking of divorcing him.
>
> As Sally brought out her hateful feelings toward her husband, she was able to see how she had turned him into a mother figure toward whom she was very ambivalent. When Sally's ambivalence toward her mother was explored in treatment and she began to experience many sexual fantasies toward her mother, Sally started to form an erotic transference toward her male therapist.
>
> In analyzing Sally's erotic transference, it became apparent that rather than experience her homosexual fantasies toward her mother, she fell in love with her male therapist and wanted to run off with him. When the therapist did not gratify any of Sally's wishes, she threatened to quit treatment. A few times she actually did leave the therapy for a week or two.
>
> What became the most crucial dynamic in understanding Sally's erotic transference were her revengeful feelings toward her mother. Just as she wished to hurt her mother for all of the frustrations she endured during her childhood, Sally wanted to hurt her therapist for his unwillingness to gratify many of her childish wishes. Said Sally to her therapist after many months of treatment, "I can't think of a better way to humiliate you, defeat you, and weaken you than to get you in bed. Instead of being a calm and competent therapist, you'll be a weakened prick."

COUNTERRESISTANCE

Just as resisting therapy at each step of the process is inevitable for the patient, so it is for the therapist. All therapists experience dangers as they work with their patients and need ways of protecting themselves. Therapists may handle their hostility toward patients by coming late for interviews habitually but rationalizing their tardiness by saying they are "behind schedule." They can cope with the anxiety that their sexual or aggressive fantasies induces by becoming overtalkative or excessively silent in sessions. Therapists have been known to develop psychosomatic responses to anxieties induced in sessions but may not always recognize that the headache, backache, or difficulty breathing is in response to the therapeutic situation.

As psychoanalytically oriented therapists have become more sensitized to the therapeutic process and view it as an exchange between two struggling human beings who are equals, they have been more willing to discuss counterresistance as a constant phenomenon in the therapeutic situation (Strean, 1993).

Therapists can resist the therapeutic process directly (for example, by coming late or cancelling appointments frequently) or indirectly (for example, by becoming drowsy in a session or making a slip while interpreting something). Their counterresistances can be "crass" or "unobtrusive." In fact, all of the resistances that we discussed in this chapter that pertain to patients are applicable to therapists. Clinicians can project parts of themselves onto the patient and use other defenses such as denial, repression, or regression in their therapeutic work (ego counterresistance). They can attempt to derive infantile gratifications from their work with patients through seductive or other manipulative behavior (id counterresistance). Therapists can feel guilty about their voyeuristic impulses, angry impulses, or other libidinal and aggressive desires that become activated during their therapeutic work (superego counterresistance). Unwittingly, they can prevent patients from growing and maturing (epinosic gain) (Strean, 1993). Finally, therapists have all kinds of transference reactions toward their patients (countertransferences) which we shall discuss in more detail.

COUNTERTRANSFERENCE

In contrast to his comprehensive and meticulous discussions of transference, Freud (1910b, 1912, 1915b, 1926) wrote very little on the subject of countertransference. He did point out that "the countertransference arises (in the analyst) as a result of the patient's influence on his unconscious feelings, and we are almost inclined to insist that he shall recognize this countertransference in himself and overcome it" (1910b, pp. 144–145). As Abend (1989) in his paper, "Countertransference and Psychoanalytic Technique" points out, "Freud's original idea that countertransference means unconscious interference with an analyst's ability to understand patients has been broadened during the past forty years: current usage often includes all of the emotional reactions at work" (p. 374). This view has received much support in the psychoanalytic literature. Slakter (1987) refers to countertransference as "all those reactions of the analyst to the patient that may help or hinder treatment" (p. 3).

Rather than viewing countertransference as a periodic unconscious interference, there is now a rather large psychoanalytic literature on countertransference with most authors acknowledging that it is as everpresent as transference and must be constantly studied by all therapists (Abend, 1989; Brenner, 1985; Greenson, 1967).

Many psychoanalytic writers (Abend, 1989; Brenner, 1985; Fine, 1982; Strean, 1991a) suggest that countertransference is a necessary prerequisite of successful psychotherapy. States Greenson (1967):

It does not do justice to the arduous demands
of the analytic profession to hope that the obtain-
ing and delivering of insight might be free from
conflict, guilt, and anxiety.   These activities
ought to be pleasurable to the analyst....   The
pleasure in listening, looking, exploring, imagining, and comprehending is not only permissible
but necessary for the optimal efficiency of the
analyst. (p. 399)

In a similar vein, Brenner (1976) states:

Whatever work one does as an adult, whatever
satisfactions one finds in a chosen profession,
whatever relationships one establishes with persons one meets with, whether in a professional
capacity or in any other, all are significantly
motivated or determined by psychic conflicts
that originated in connection with childhood
instinctual wishes. One cannot, therefore, distinguish sharply between countertransference
that deserves to be called normal and that which
deserves to be called pathological. Just as in the
case of neurotic symptoms, the differences (between the neurotic and normal) are a matter of
degree. (p. 130)

Examples of Countertransference

Positive countertransference

Psychotherapy usually proceeds well when the therapist
likes the patient. Although positive countertransference is
a desirable attitude like a positive transference, it should be
studied carefully (Fine, 1982).

If a patient is loved too much, the therapist will tend to
overidentify with him or her and not be able to help the
patient see his or her role in writing neurotic scripts,
particularly those scripts that pertain to troubled interper-

sonal relationships. Overidentification frequently takes place in working on marital and parent-child conflicts.

> Ron Masefield was a married man in his early 40s who sought therapy because he got into constant arguments with his wife. As Ron described his conflicts with his wife and talked about how she was "so similar" to his "controlling and mean" mother, his female therapist felt a great deal of sympathy for him. Slowly she began to be quite critical of Ron's wife and mother. As she did so, Ron felt very "supported" and "vindicated." However, his arguments with his wife intensified and eventually he and his wife separated. Ron told his therapist, "I felt that you were my ally in the war and every time I was in a fight with my wife, you were the gun I needed."

Ron never did get to learn much about his unresolved problems with women. What he did get from therapy was "a gun!"

> Shirley North was seen in a child guidance clinic to discuss her troubles with her teenage daughter. As Ms. North described her bitter battles with her daughter, her male therapist found himself resenting the daughter. Slowly and in a raised voice he instructed Ms. North how to limit her daughter. However, Ms. North sensed the therapist's rancor, told him he was "hypercritical" and left treatment.

If the practitioner is overidentified with the patient, the patient can feel subtly encouraged to act out as was true in the case of Ron Masefield. Another response to the therapist's overidentification is the patient feeling misunderstood. He or she can then quit treatment as was true of Ms. North.

Negative countertransference

Although patients often have difficulty acknowledging
their hostile feelings toward the therapist, therapists have
even more difficulty acknowledging their hostility toward
their patients. Yet, therapists are human beings and can
become frustrated by the patient's lack of progress, pro-
voked by the patient's accusations and dissatisfactions, or
bored by the patient's constant complaints. Because mental health practitioners are "not supposed" to feel hostile,
their hostile feelings toward patients are often disguised
and repressed; then these feelings manifest themselves in
subtle forms in and out of the therapy. Two of the most
common expressions of disguised hostility are the use of
the clinical diagnosis as a countertransference expression
and alterations of therapeutic plans and procedures (Fine,
1982).

> Ms. Judith Love, a 44-year-old divorced woman,
> was in intensive therapy for depression, work
> dissatisfaction, and unsuccessful relationships
> with men. After finding her first consultation
> with her male therapist "very encouraging," she
> rather quickly changed her mind about him in
> the third interview when he was wearing a suit
> that "was out of fashion." As her criticisms
> mounted and her therapist felt irritated with her,
> the therapist found himself referring to Judith
> Love as "a phallic character." Still later when
> Judith became even more vituperative and resis-
> tive, the therapist concluded that she was a
> "borderline."
> Every couple of months the therapist changed
> his clinical diagnosis, making it more and more
> severe as his patient became more critical of him.
> After about 7 months of treatment, Judith Love
> was diagnosed as "an ambulatory schizophrenic."
> In the 8th month of treatment, she was consid-
> ered "openly psychotic and psychopathic." Af-

ter 10 months of therapy, Judith Love was diag-
nosed as "untreatable." That was when she quit
treatment.

When patients are critical of the therapist, isolate themselves from a relationship with him or her, do not get better
and/or regress, therapists often blame the therapeutic
modality they are using and keep on changing it.

When Barry King, a married man in his 30s
who came for help with his difficult marriage,
was not making progress in his individual treatment, his therapist suggested conjoint marital
counseling with Barry's wife. When Mr. and Mrs.
King spent their time arguing, the therapist separated them, and saw each of them in individual
treatment. When that didn't work and family
therapy was suggested, the Kings dropped out of
treatment, feeling they were "too difficult to help."

Very often when a patient does not move in therapy, the
negative transference is not being sufficiently examined.
The reason for this omission by therapists is that they do
not want to face anger in themselves toward the patient.
When therapists cannot face something in themselves,
they usually cannot help their patients face the same issue.

ACTIVITIES OF THE PSYCHOANALYTICALLY
ORIENTED THERAPIST

One of the primary tasks of the analytically oriented
therapist is to *listen*. As the patient produces material,
themes emerge and the therapist *asks questions* so that
persistent themes receive further elaboration. As certain
resistances and transference reactions become clear to the
practitioner, the therapist *confronts* the patient with them,
that is, draws the patient's attention to a particular phe-

nomenon, such as lateness to appointments, and tries to help the patient face what has not been faced about himself or herself.

Clarification involves bringing the details about what has been confronted into sharper focus. It involves "digging out" significant details from the past that are being recapitulated in the present. Following confrontation and clarification is *interpretation*. This involves providing meaning to the patient's thoughts, feelings, fantasies, dreams, and behavior. Its goal is self-understanding or *insight*. *Working through* is the integration of understanding by repeating and deepening insights. Finally, the patient *synthesizes* the insights by working out an adequate way of coping with life so that work and love are more fully enjoyed.

Listening

It usually takes many years of experience for a therapist to have a strong conviction that empathetic listening without talking is very much what contributes the most to a patient's getting better. Practitioners often forget that when people discuss their problems with others, the latter are quick to give reassurance and advice so that tensions are not discharged and the person under stress feels devalued. Patients begin to value themselves much more when their therapists value what they say. This can only take place if the recipient of therapy has as a therapist a quiet, nonintrusive, empathetic listener.

Asking Questions

One of the central procedures in good interviewing is posing good questions. A question that truly engages the patient is one that clarifies ambiguities, completes a picture of the situation being described, obtains more detail about the patient's thinking, and elicits emotional responses (Kadushin, 1972).

Questions have to be phrased so that they can be understood. They should be unambiguous and simple enough for the patient to remember what is being asked. Questions that can be answered with "no" or "yes" do not really help the person to discharge feelings and tensions nor relate facts. If a patient is asked, "Do you like your boss?" he or she is given little opportunity to really reflect on attitudes toward the boss. However, if the patient is asked, "Can you tell me about your boss?" the chance of more data being elicited is enhanced.

Above all, the patient, to address a question, must feel that it comes from an interested and empathetic questioner. Otherwise, there is little motivation to become involved in the therapy.

Confrontation

In order to help patients learn about those forces that are contributing to their unhappiness, they have to be confronted from time to time with behavior of which they are unaware and/or has not been addressed by them. When confronting a patient with a piece of behavior, such as missed sessions, lateness, ignoring the therapist's comments, or ingratiating remarks, the therapist has to be sure that there is sufficient data available to make a firm statement about the issue. The phenomenon to be addressed, for example, lateness, should have occurred repeatedly before it is raised in the therapy; otherwise, there is a good chance the patient will not relate to the confrontation.

As Greenson (1967) suggests, premature demonstrations of resistive or transferential behavior is not only a waste of time, but often compounds anxiety, intensifies resistance, and dissipates material that might be better assimilated at a later point in the therapy.

> After 5 months of treatment with Bill Josephs, a man in his 30s, it became clear to his male tharapist that after Bill would say he was being helped, he would miss his next session. When the therapist confronted Bill with his behavior, Bill at first felt it was insignificant and offered several rationalizations to account for his missed sessions. When the therapist showed Bill how much he was avoiding the therapist's confrontation in the here-and-now, Bill again moved away. He told the therapist that the latter wanted "too much intimacy" and that he, Bill, was not interested.
>
> In effect, Bill demonstrated that the therapist's confrontation was correct but unacceptable to him.

Clarification

Obviously, it is insufficient for a patient just to be aware of a piece of behavior, such as missing sessions. Patients should understand why they are behaving the way they do.

> Bill Josephs, in the above example, needed help in *clarifying* why intimacy was something that "did not interest" him. His therapist asked him what bothered him about closeness and intimacy and learned that Bill felt powerless, weakened, and subordinate in a close relationship. This was what he felt with his parents and brother. To be close was to be "crushed," according to Bill Josephs.

Interpretation

Interpretation is that activity that makes the patient aware of the unconscious meaning, source, history, mode, or cause of a given psychic event. Interpretations can only be given after the patient has been confronted with a phenomenon, issue, or attitude, some clarification has ensued, and the therapist feels that the patient has some conviction about the matter within himself or herself.

By the time Freud came to write his papers on technique, he began to distinguish between the content of an interpretation and its communication to the patient. In 1926 Freud wrote:

> When you have found the right interpretation, another task lies ahead. You must wait for the right moment at which you can communicate your interpretation to the patient with some prospect of success....You will be making a bad mistake if you throw your interpretations at the patient's head as soon as you have found them. (p. 160)

Interpretation in the psychoanalytic literature has come to have a variety of meanings (Sandler, et. al, 1973):

1. The analyst's inferences and conclusions regarding the unconscious meaning and significance of the patient's communication and behavior.
2. The communication by the analyst of these inferences and conclusions.
3. All comments made by the analyst—confrontations, clarifications, questions, and so on.
4. Verbal interventions specifically aimed at bringing about dynamic change through insight.

Fine (1982) suggested that there are three types of interpretation: uncovering, connective, and integrative.

The uncovering interpretation is one through which a concealed wish is brought to consciousness.

> After Bill Josephs, talked a great deal about his dread of closeness and detailed some history that contributed to it, the therapist made the uncovering interpretation about Bill's missed sessions: "If you come to every session, you are afraid you will bring us too close and that will be too uncomfortable for you."

In the connective interpretation, the present is related to the past so that the patient can see how he or she is distorting the present by waging old battles and seeking childish gratifications.

> In working on Bill Joseph's missed appointments, the therapist later made a connective interpretation and pointed out that Bill had turned the therapist into his father and brother and was afraid that the therapist would crush and demean him.

The integrative interpretation involves pulling together material from a variety of sources in order to help the patient see his or her problems in a fuller perspective.

> In helping Bill Josephs, the therapist repeatedly showed him how he was keeping himself as a child in his interpersonal relationships, making others much bigger and then running away.

Repeated interpretations of resistance, transferences, and other behaviors is what is meant by *working through*. More *insight* is gained and a *synthesis* evolves.

The decisive question with regard to the therapist's activities is not whether a confrontation, clarification, or interpretation is correct, but how the patient reacts to it and what the therapist does with it.

Patients tend to respond to interventions in terms of their unique dynamics and current transferences to the therapist. Often their response to an interpretation is of more importance than anything else. A patient's continual compliance to an interpretation may be more crucial to understand than how well he or she understands the content of the interpretation. The same would be true of a patient's consistent belligerence, ambivalence, or any other response to an intervention.

The therapeutic situation is a dynamic dialogue. In this dialogue the patient's responses to the therapist's interventions must always be scrutinized. The primary focus in psychoanalytically oriented psychotherapy is on the ways in which the patient responds to interventions, rather than on whether the content is correct or incorrect.

RECOMMENDED READINGS

The most lucid and comprehensive book on the technique of psychoanalytically oriented therapy is Greenson's *The Technique and Practice of Psychoanalysis.* Also of much value, particularly to the beginning therapist, is Fine's *Healing of the Mind.* For a clear discussion of the history of psychoanalytic technique from Freud to the present, see Bergmann and Hartman's *The Evolution of Psychoanalytic Technique.*

An interesting and creative discussion of the psychoanalytic process, can be found in Roy Schafer's *The Analytic Attitude* and *Retelling a Life.* For an excellent and honest discussion of countertransference issues, see

Searle's is *Countertransference and Related Subjects.*
Strean examines countertransference reactions in the analytic situation, in *Behind the Couch.*

Strean also discusses resistances and counterresistances, in *Resolving Resistances in Psychotherapy* and *Resolving Counterrestances in Psychotherapy.* For a brilliant exposition on how to relate technique to the patient, see Brenner's *Psychoanalytic Technique and Psychic Conflict.*

A collection of some of the major articles on countertransference starting with Freud and extending through the 1970s may be found in Epstein and Feiner's *Countertransference: The Therapist's Contribution to the Therapeutic Situation.*

5

PSYCHOANALYSIS AND RESEARCH

Evaluation of psychoanalysis as a form of therapeutic intervention has been taking place almost since the inception of the discipline. Freud wrote up many cases in which he evaluated his treatment results, and his contemporaries did likewise (Jones, 1957). In the first major study of the results of psychoanalytic treatment, Fenichel (1930) reviewed the work at the Berlin Psychoanalytic Institute. He reported that about 60% of the patients studied markedly improved. Jones (1937) reviewed the psychoanalytic treatment at the London Psychoanalytic Institute from 1926 to 1936 and reported findings similar to Fenichel. Studies by Alexander (1938) at the Chicago Institute for Psychoanalysis from 1932 to 1937, by Kessel and Hyman (1933) who published a survey of patients treated by a variety of analysts from the early 1920s to 1933, and a study by Feldman (1968) at the Southern California Institute have all yielded results similar to those mentioned.

In one of the most intensive studies that compared psychoanalytic treatment to psychoanalytically oriented psychotherapy, Wallerstein (1986) demonstrated that these two therapeutic modalities achieved positive results similar to those studies mentioned above. Wallerstein's methodology was much more rigorous than those used in the previous studies. In contrast to the aforementioned research, Wallerstein used ratings of judges, recording devices, follow-up interviews, and a variety of other research instruments.

IS THE RESEARCH ON PSYCHOANALYTICALLY ORIENTED TREATMENT VALID?

Although psychoanalytically oriented psychotherapy has been subjected to evaluation on numerous occasions, and although the studies in the literature report that between 50 to 75% of the patients terminated treatment markedly improved (Alexander, 1938; Feldman, 1968; Fenichel, 1930; Ferenczi, 1955; Jones, 1937; Wallerstein, 1986), these research results have been questioned and continue to be questioned. Because of the absence of control groups and the possible bias of the investigators—who may have wanted to prove that the treatment is effective because of their psychoanalytic orientation—many writers have challenged the results of psychoanalytic research.

Jerome Frank (1961) pointed out that psychoanalytically oriented therapists have considerable emotional investment in their method:

> His self esteem, status, and financial security are linked to its effectiveness. Under these circumstances he can hardly be expected to be an impartial student of his own method, and any data he reports cannot escape the suspicion of bias. (p. 226)

Eysenck (1952, 1966), a behaviorist, was one of the first researchers to challenge the effectiveness of psychoanalytic therapy. Contending that available evidence does not adequately support the claim that psychoanalysis is therapeutically effective, Eysenck claimed to have telling evidence that psychoanalysis did no better than simply having people go without therapy. Eysenck's argument may be summarized as follows:

1. If there is no adequate study of psychoanalytic therapy showing an improvement rate of better than two thirds or better than that of a suitable no-treatment control group, then there is no firm evidence that the therapy is therapeutically effective.
2. There is no adequate study showing either rate of improvement.
3. Therefore, there is no firm evidence that the therapy is effective. (Erwin, 1980)

In a review of the subsequent literature on the effectiveness of psychoanalytic treatment, Grunbaum (1977) concluded that the superiority of the outcome of analytic treatment over rival therapies has not been demonstrated. In his essay, "How Scientific Is Psychoanalysis?" Grunbaum points out that if psychoanalytic treatment outcomes do exceed the spontaneous remission rate, this alone does not suffice to establish that psychoanalytic treatment gains are due to psychoanalytic intervention. It would not rule out that such treatment gains are due to a placebo effect. In his reviews of the pertinent literature on treatment effectiveness, Grunbaum concludes that there is good reason to suspect that insofar as Freudian therapy is effective, it is "placebogenic." He further suggests (1) psychotherapy of a wide variety of types and for a broad range of disorders is better than nothing, but (2) there is either no difference between different therapeutic modalities or perhaps treatment other than psychoanalytic is superior.

Many writers (Grunbaum, 1984; Spence, 1981) quarrel with the use of clinical evidence as support for psychoanalytic treatment because it always consists of data subject to investigator bias. As Von Eckardt (1985) suggests,

> Not only are the data being gathered in the
> clinical setting obtained by someone firmly com-
> mitted to the truth of the theory, but they are
> gathered in such a way—during the course of a
> therapeutic process in which transference plays a
> major role—that even Freud worried about the
> charge of suggestion. (p. 394)

Another criticism of the research on psychoanalysis is
that there is no *experimental proof* of any of the doctrines
of psychoanalysis. Most of the treatment examined and
most of the personality theory evaluated has not been
quantified. (Hall and Lindzey, 1957)

The Data of Psychoanalysis Are Not Easily Reproducible

In his book *The Psychoanalytic Vision*, Reuben Fine (1981)
points out that the data of psychoanalysis—dreams, fantasies, slips of the tongue, transference, resistance, neurotic
symptoms, and so forth—cannot be quantified in a way
that will satisfy experimental psychologists. Consequently,
experimental psychologists and other researchers have
tended to write off psychoanalysis as unscientific. Fine
suggests that to research psychoanalysis, one will always
have to rely on unquantifiable clinical data. This same
view was suggested 25 years earlier by the eminent experimental psychologist Boring (1957), who said:

> Apparently psychology is not in a position to
> validate or invalidate psychoanalysis experimen-
> tally—with selected groups and carefully chosen
> controls. Hence, we are reduced to the collection of
> case histories. (p. 10)

PSYCHOANALYSTS RESPOND TO CRITICISMS OF
THEIR RESEARCH

Some psychoanalysts have begun to respond to the many
experimental psychologists and other researchers who

have attacked their discipline because it is "too anecdotal" and/or "unscientific." Fine (1983) in *The Logic of Psychology: A Dynamic Approach* suggested that psychoanalysis as a theoretical structure should be regarded as a scientific systematic psychology.

> Its major ingredients are naturalistic observation and integration of material from many different sources. When looked at in this way, it is seen that psychoanalysis really represents the heart of psychology; without some reference to psychodynamics no psychological statement makes complete sense. A careful examination of some recent psychological literature shows that current "scientific psychology" as usually seen by academicians is often either irrelevant or trivial or erroneous. A total rethinking of the science in the light of psychoanalytic psychology is essential. Then it will be clear that psychology, based on psychoanalysis, also embraces history, anthropology, economics, literary criticism, and all the other sciences that deal with man. (p. 203)

Fine, in effect, has taken the position that is quite popular among psychoanalysts: an examination of cases in which the dynamics are well understood is science. This view suggests that statistics and psychoanalysis are strange bedfellows.

In a review of the work of the psychoanalyst Merton Gill, Irwin Hoffman (1985) reports on Gill's unwavering commitment to the necessity of systematic research on the psychoanalytic process.

Hoffman points out that Gill "has never accepted the common psychoanalytic view, which Freud himself promulgated, that the case study method...can obviate the need for a more rigorous application of scientific methods to the gathering and analysis of psychoanalytic data" (p. 168). One of Gill's most important contributions to the development of psychoanalysis as a science is his attempt to make the raw data of psychoanalysis available for study by independent observers through audio recordings of psychoanalytic sessions.

Hoffman (1985) points out that Gill's theory of technique is also congenial to research on the psychoanalytic process in that it invites attention to each analytic hour as a unit that has an integrity of meaning. One of the fruits of Gill's commitment to systematic research has been the development of a coding scheme that permits classification of various kinds of patient communications and analyst interventions.

In a recent book, *Psychoanalysis As a Science*, Leopold Bellak (1993) demonstrates the fact that many psychoanalytic hypotheses are experimentally verifiable, publicly demonstrable, and repeatable. He shows how experimentally controlled research can demonstrate the validity of a concept such as projection, or how treatment progress can be measured in psychoanalytic therapy. Bellak's major contribution is to operationalize personality and treatment concepts to measure them empirically.

In the same book, Bellak (1993) succeeds in providing logical links between psychoanalytic interpretation and psychological theory as Fine (1983) prescribed. Bellak was able to demonstrate that psychoanalysis is a theory of learning, of perception, and of communication. To answer the many critics of psychoanalytic research, Bellak details some of the interesting opportunities technology offers for enhancing psychoanalytic research by utilizing word processors and video recordings.

PROBLEMS IN PSYCHOANALYTIC RESEARCH: A SUMMARY

As the reader is now no doubt aware, there are many problems in psychoanalytic research, most of which are probably applicable to all clinical research. Many, if not all, of the following problems have not been resolved, although psychoanalysts and other clinicians are discussing and debating them much more than they did heretofore.

The first problem in doing research on psychoanalytic treatment (or any other therapy) begins with a decision on what ails the patient. Patients may feel that what ails them is their spouse, whereas their therapists may feel that what ails their patients are unresolved sexual and aggressive problems. A group of independent judges may arrive at some other definition of the problems. Therefore, one of the difficulties in doing clinical research is establishing what "problem" is being researched, according to whose definition.

A corollary of the above issue is that because it is very difficult to accurately describe the nature of maladaptive behavior, it is often an onerous task to collect a group of patients with similar problems so that the influence of a given treatment can be scientifically evaluated. For example, two individuals can have food addictions. Neither of them or one of them may refer to the problem as food addiction and their therapists may or may not agree with their patients' definitions of their problems. Furthermore, as we have discussed in previous chapters, the same presenting problem, food addiction, may be a regressive problem for one patient and a fixation for the other. Thus, it is difficult to do psychoanalytic research when the subjects of the study are so very different from one another.

Another problem in researching psychoanalytic treatment is in defining the exact nature of the intervention utilized, that is, the independent variable. As discussed in Chapter 4, patients and therapists unconsciously perceive each other's overt behavior in ways that are often difficult for the research to unearth. For example, if in a particular therapy hour the therapist presents an interpretation, the impact of this interpretation on the patient may not be apparent to the researcher: many variables have been affecting the patient prior to the interpretation, which can influence the patient in many ways and which even he or she may not be sure about. As Herma (1963) pointed out, the number of variables involved in a therapeutic hour inevitably present a virtually impossible task for the scientific statistician.

Often many events occur with such split-second rapidity that an analyst or therapist can integrate them all, especially when the practitioner is under pressure to make some therapeutic response. Also, the practitioner at these moments may be too close to the events to judge their significance, so that the selection of the practitioner may result in serious omissions (Colby, 1960).

Scientists inevitably point out that observations, if they are to be considered useful, cannot be haphazard or chancy. In science, systematic observations are guided by a specific hypothesis that organizes observations and links them to specific concerns.

In psychotherapeutic research we are forced to select variables relevant to a hypothesis concerning the problem to be studied. Suppose we are interested in the patient's anxiety. It is extremely difficult, if not impossible, *to be sure* that we are observing anxiety when we think so. Sometimes researchers (for example, Bellak, 1993) assign units of motor, verbal, or affective behaviors to measure anxiety. The problem is that the above referents may be measuring other variables beside anxiety. Hence, the validity of the study might be negatively affected.

Another requirement of the scientist is that systematic observations must be recorded. As we mentioned earlier, it is well known that when therapists record, it influences their therapeutic behavior—for no other reason than the fact that attention is being withdrawn from the therapeutic process. Perhaps of more pertinence, when patients observe the therapist taking notes, this too inevitably affects the patient's behavior in the treatment situation.

Some researchers feel that tape or television recordings obviate the problems that occur in reporting. However, being on TV or audiotape certainly influences the productions of both therapist and patient.

In *Psychoanalytic Research*, Colby (1960) points out that in all clinical research it is important to scrutinize our activity to make sure that we are counting negative as well as positive instances of our hypotheses. Multiple independent observers have been utilized to serve as one means of scrutinizing therapeutic activity. However, the assumption underlying the use of independent observers is that they are capable of genuine independent judgments. As Colby points out, and as the eminent clinical researcher Hans Strupp (1977) reinforces, observers might agree only because they share the same conceptual biases and not because of what exists in external reality—a point we have reiterated throughout this chapter.

The final problem in clinical research that we have alluded to but stress further is what Fine (1983) has called "the measurement problem."

One of the most difficult dimensions of research in psychotherapy is measurement. If one looks solely at external behavior, there is little problem. Many behaviorists (for example, Eysenck, 1966) have stated that goals and objectives should be "symptom oriented" and posed in such a manner that their attainment is measurable. However, for those clinicians who view the human being as a complex biological, psychological, and social organism, measurement poses considerable problems. If the therapist believes that hopes, dreams, emotions, fantasies, and other internal states are important data, then research activities must take these phenomena into account.

The difficulty with much research on human beings, and with human beings in the therapy situation, is that it must take into account introspective data. If one human being asks another a question, the answer is a variable one. It depends on the question, on the relationship between the questioner and the one being questioned (that is, the transference–countertransference relationship), and on many other subjective, introspective factors. If an individual introspects, the nature and meaning of his or her findings are variable.

Few theories, with the exception of psychoanalytic theory, take into full account the measurement problem (Fine, 1983). As has been demonstrated in previous chapters, this perspective allows for internal motives and recognizes that what a subject tells the experimenter in an experiment—whether the experiment involves written questionnaires or oral interviews—depends on the relationship between the two, that is, it depends on transference and countertransference reactions.

Unless motivation of the subjects is taken into account in clinical research, the observations will be contaminated. The fact that certain types of behavior can be enumerated, whereas motives cannot, does not imply that solid research should dispense with such an important dimension of the human being.

Throughout this book we have reiterated that psychoanalysis is a theory of personality, a perspective on psychopathology, an orientation to therapy, and a means of research. As a theory of personality, most would agree it is comprehensive, informative, and clear. As a perspective on psychopathology, it is accepted by many mental health professionals and lay persons as explanatory too. As a therapy, it is not as well accepted by many because research in its present state cannot easily validate the results.

RECOMMENDED READING

For the most up-to-date and comprehensive text on research in psychoanalysis, Bellak's book, *Psychoanalysis*

As a Science is highly recommended. For excellent arguments against quantifying research in psychoanalysis, yet viewing psychoanalysis as a science, see Fine's *The Logic of Psychology.*

To clarify some of the methodological problems in psychoanalytic research, see Colby's *Psychoanalytic Research.* For a comprehensive and lucid discussion of research in psychotherapy in general, see Hans Strupp's *Psychotherapy for Better or Worse.*

For a research-oriented argument against psychoanalysis from a brilliant philosopher, see Grunbaum's *The Foundations of Psychoanalysis: A Philosophical Critique.*

An excellent piece of research that pays close attention to the consumer's view of psychotherapy is Strupp, Fox, and Lesser's *Patients View Their Psychotherapy.*

BIBLIOGRAPHY

Abend, S. (1989). Countertransference and psychoanalytic technique. *The Psychoanalytic Quarterly, 58,* 374–395.

Adler, A. (1927). *The practice and theory of individual psychology.* New York: Harcourt.

Adler, A. (1929). *Problems of neurosis.* London: Kegan Paul.

Adler, A. (1941). Individual Psychology. In C. Murchison (Ed.), *Psychologies of 1930.* Worcester, MA: Clark University Press.

Alexander, F. (1938). *Five year report of the Chicago Institute for Psychoanalysis 1932–1937.* Chicago: Chicago Institute for Psychoanalysis.

Alexander, F., Eisenstein, S., & Grotjahn, M. (1965). *Psychoanalytic pioneers.* New York: Basic Books.

Ansbacher, H. & Ansbacher, R. (1956). *The individual psychology of Alfred Adler.* New York: Basic Books.

Appignanesi, L. & Forrester, J. (1992). *Freud's women.* New York: Basic Books.

Bellak, L. (1993). *Psychoanalysis as a science.* Boston: Allyn and Bacon.

Bergmann, M. & Hartman, F. (1976). *The evolution of psychoanalytic technique.* New York: Basic Books.

Berthelsdorf, S. (1976). Survey of the successful analysis of a young man addicted to heroin. In *Psychoanalytic Study of the Child,* 3l, 165–192.

Bion, W. (1955). Language and the schizophrenic. In M. Klein, P. Heimann, & R. Money-Kryle (Eds.), *New directions in psychoanalysis.* New York: Basic Books.

Boring, E. (1957). *A history of experimental psychology.* New York: Appleton-Century-Crofts.

Brenner, C. (1955). *An elementary textbook of psychoanalysis.* New York: International Universities Press.

Brenner, C. (1976). *Psychoanalytic technique and psychic conflict.* New York: International Universities Press.

Brenner, C. (1985). Countertransference as compromise formation. *The Psychoanalytic Quarterly, 54,* 155–l63.

Briehl, W. (1966). Wilhelm Reich—Character analysis. In F. Alexander, S. Eisenstein, & M. Grotjahn (Eds.), *Psychoanalytic pioneers.* New York: Basic Books.

Cameron, N. (1963). *Personality development and psychopathology.* New York: Houghton Mifflin Company.

Clark, R. (1980). *Freud: The man and the cause.* New York: Random House.

Colby, K. (1960). *Psychoanalytic research.* New York: Basic Books.

Corsini, R. (1973). *Current psychotherapies.* Itasca, IL: F. E. Peacock Publishers, Inc.

English, O. & Pearson, G. (1945). *Emotional problems of living.* New York: W. W. Norton and Co.

Epstein, L. & Feiner, A. (1979). *Countertransference: The therapist's contribution to the therapeutic situation.* New York: Jason Aronson.

Erikson, E. (1950). *Childhood and society.* New York: W. W. Norton.

Erikson, E. (1959). Identity and the life cycle. *Psychological Issues. Monograph I.* New York: International Universities Press.

Erikson, E. (1964). *Insight and responsibility.* New York: W. W. Norton.

Erwin, E. (1980). Psychoanalytic therapy: The Eysenck argument. *American Psychologist, 35,* 435–443.

Eysenck, H. (1952). The effects of psychotherapy: An evaluation. *Journal of Consulting Psychology, 16,* 319–324.

Eysenck, H. (1966). *The effects of psychotherapy.* New York: International Science Press.

Fairbairn, W. (1952). *Psychoanalytic studies of the personality.* London: Tavistock.

Feldman, F. (1968). Results of psychoanalysis in clinic case assignments. *Journal of the American Psychoanalytic Association, 16,* 274–300.

Fenichel, O. (1930). *Zehn Jahre Berliner Psychoanalytisches Institut.* Vienna: International Psychoanalytisches Verlag.

Fenichel, O. (1945). *The psychoanalytic theory of neurosis.* New York: W. W. Norton.

Ferenczi, S. (1955). The problem of the termination of the analysis. In *Final contributions to the problems and methods of psychoanalysis.* New York: Basic Books.

Fine, R. (1962). *Freud: A critical re-evaluation of his theories.* New York: David McKay Company.

Fine, R. (1973). Psychoanalysis. In R. Corsini (Ed.), *Current psychotherapies.* Itasca, IL: F. E. Peacock, Publishers.

Fine, R. (1975). *Psychoanalytic psychology.* New York: Jason Aronson.

Fine, R. (1979). *A history of psychoanalysis.* New York: Columbia University Press.

Fine, R. (1981). *The psychoanalytic vision.* New York: The Free Press.

Fine, R. (1982). *The healing of the mind.* (2nd ed.). New York: The Free Press.

Fine, R. (1983). *The logic of psychology.* Washington, DC: University Press of America.

Fine, R. (1989). *Current and historical perspectives on the borderline patient.* New York: Brunner/Mazel.

Fine, R. (1990). *Love and work.* New York: Continuum.

Frank, J. (1961). *Persuasion and healing.* Baltimore: Johns Hopkins Press.

Freeman, L. & Strean, H. (1987). *Freud and women.* New York: Continuum.

Freud, A. (1946). *The ego and the mechanisms of defense.* New York: International Universities Press.

Freud, A. (1965). *Normality and pathology in childhood: Assessment of development.* New York: International Universities Press.

Freud, A. & Burlingham, D. (1943a). *War and children.* New York: Medical War Books.

Freud, A. & Burlingham, D. (1943b). *Infants without families.* New York: International Universities Press.

Freud, S. (1896). Further remarks on the neuro-psychoses of defense. In J. Strachey (Ed. & Trans.), *The standard edition of the complete psychological works of Sigmund Freud* (Vol. 3, pp. 157–185). London: Hogarth Press.

Freud, S. (1900). The interpretation of dreams. In J. Strachey (Ed. & Trans.), *The standard edition of the complete psychological works of Sigmund Freud* (Vol. 4, pp.7–338). London: Hogarth Press.

Freud, S. (1904). Freud's psychoanalytic procedure. In J. Strachey (Ed. & Trans.), *The standard edition of the complete psychological works of Sigmund Freud* (Vol. 7, pp. 249–256). London: Hogarth Press.

Freud, S. (1905). Three essays on the theory of sexuality. In J. Strachey (Ed. & Trans.), *The standard edition of the complete psychological works of Sigmund Freud* (Vol. 7, pp. 125–248). London: Hogarth Press.

Freud, S. (1910a). Wild psychoanalysis. In J. Strachey (Ed. & Trans.), *The standard edition of the complete psychological works of Sigmund Freud* (Vol. 11, pp. 141–151). London: Hogarth Press.

Freud, S. (1910b). The future prospects of psycho-analytic therapy. In J. Strachey (Ed. & Trans.), *The standard edition of the complete psychological works of Sigmund Freud* (Vol. 11, pp. 139–151). London: Hogarth Press.

Freud, S. (1912). The dynamics of transference. In J. Strachey (Ed. & Trans.), *The standard edition of the complete psychological works of Sigmund Freud* (Vol. 12, pp. 97–108). London: Hogarth Press.

Freud, S. (1913a). On beginning the treatment. In J. Strachey (Ed. & Trans.), *The standard edition of the complete psychological works of Sigmund Freud* (Vol.12, pp.121–144). London: Hogarth Press.

Freud, S. (1913b). Totem and taboo. In J. Strachey (Ed. & Trans.), *The standard edition of the complete psychologi-*

cal works of Sigmund Freud (Vol. 13, pp.1–162). London: Hogarth Press.

Freud, S. (1914a). Remembering, repeating, and working through. In J. Strachey (Ed.& Trans.), *The standard edition of the complete psychological works of Sigmund Freud* (Vol. 12, pp. 145–156). London: Hogarth Press.

Freud, S. (1914b). On narcissism: An introduction. In J. Strachey (Ed. & Trans.), *The standard edition of the complete psychological works of Sigmund Freud* (Vol. 14, pp. 67–l04). London: Hogarth Press.

Freud, S. (1915a). The unconscious. In J. Strachey (Ed. & Trans.), *The standard edition of the complete psychological works of Sigmund Freud* (Vol. 14, pp. 159–216) London: Hogarth Press.

Freud, S. (1915b). Observations on transference love. In J. Strachey (Ed. & Trans.), *The standard edition of the complete psychological works of Sigmund Freud* (Vol. 12, pp. 157–171). London: Hogarth Press.

Freud, S. (1916). Some character types met with in psychoanalytic work. In J. Strachey (Ed. & Trans.), *The standard edition of the complete psychological works of Sigmund Freud* (Vol. 14, pp. 309–333). London: Hogarth Press.

Freud, S. (1917). Analytic therapy. In J. Strachey (Ed. & Trans.), *The standard edition of the complete psychological works of Sigmund Freud* (Vol. 16, pp. 448–463). London: Hogarth Press.

Freud, S. (1919). Lines of advance in psychoanalytic therapy. In J. Strachey (Ed. & Trans.), *The standard edition of the complete psychological works of Sigmund Freud* (Vol. 17, pp. 139–168). London: Hogarth Press.

Freud, S. (1923). The ego and the id. In J. Strachey (Ed. & Trans.), *The standard edition of the complete psychological works of Sigmund Freud* (Vol. 19, pp. 1–66). London: Hogarth Press.

Freud, S. (1926). Inhibitions, symptoms, and anxiety. In J. Strachey (Ed. & Trans.), *The standard edition of the complete psychological works of Sigmund Freud* (Vol. 20, pp. 77–174). London: Hogarth Press.

Freud, S. (1933). New introductory lectures. In J. Strachey (Ed. & Trans.), *The standard edition of the complete psychological works of Sigmund Freud* (Vol. 22, pp. 1–182). London: Hogarth Press.

Freud, S. (1937). Analysis terminable and interminable. In J. Strachey (Ed. & Trans.), *The standard edition of the complete psychological works of Sigmund Freud* (Vol. 23, pp. 209–253). London: Hogarth Press.

Freud, S. (1938). *The basic writings of Sigmund Freud*. New York: Random House (Modern Library).

Freud, S. (1939). An outline of psychoanalysis. In J. Strachey (Ed. & Trans.), *The standard edition of the complete psychological works of Sigmund Freud* (Vol. 23, pp. 139–251). London: Hogarth Press.

Friedman, R. (1988). *Male homosexuality: A contemporary psychoanalytic perspective*. New Haven, CT: Yale University Press.

Gay, P. (1988). *Freud: A life for our time*. New York: W.W. Norton.

Glover, E. (1949). *Psychoanalysis*. London: Staples Press.

Glover, E. (1955). *The technique of psychoanalysis*. New York: International Universities Press.

Glover, E. (1960). *The roots of crime*. New York: International Universities Press.

Greenson, R. (1967). *The technique and practice of psychoanalysis*. New York: International Universities Press.

Grotstein, J. (1966). Projective identification in the therapeutic process. *International Journal of Psychoanalysis, 47,* 26–31.

Grunbaum, A. (1977). How scientific is psychoanalysis? In R. Stern, L. Horowitz, & J. Lynes (Eds.), *Science and psychotherapy,* (pp. 219–254). New York: Haven Press.

Grunbaum, A. (1984). *The foundations of psychoanalysis: A philosophical critique*. Berkeley: University of California Press.

Hall, C. & Lindzey, G. (1957). *Theories of personality.* New York: John Wiley and Sons.

Hartmann, H. (1958). *Ego psychology and the problem of adaptation.* New York: International Universities Press.

Hartmann, H. (1964). *Essays on ego psychology.* New York: International Universities Press.

Herma, H. (1963). *A handbook of psychoanalysis.* New York: World Publishing Company.

Hoffman, I. (1985). Merton M. Gill: A study in theory development. In J. Reppen (Ed.), *Beyond Freud.* Hillsdale, NJ: The Analytic Press.

Horney, K. (1937). *The neurotic personality of our time.* New York: W. W. Norton.

Horney, K. (1945). *Our inner conflicts.* New York: W. W. Norton.

Horney, K. (1950). *Neurosis and human growth.* New York: W. W. Norton.

Horney, K. (1967). *Feminine psychology.* New York: W. W. Norton.

Isay, R. (1989). *Being homosexual: Gay men and their development.* New York: Farrar, Straus & Giroux.

Jacobson, E. (1953). Contribution to the metapsychology of cyclothymic depression. In P. Greenacre (Ed.), *Affective disorders.* New York: International Universities Press.

Jones, E. (1937). *Decennial report of the London Clinic of Psychoanalysis.* London: London Institute of Psychoanalysis.

Jones, E. (1957). *The life and work of Sigmund Freud* (3 vol.). New York: Basic Books.

Jung, C. (1915). *The theory of psychoanalysis.* New York: Nervous and Mental Disease Publishing Company.

Jung, C. (1917). *Collected papers on analytical psychology.* New York: Moffat, Yard.

Jung, C. (1918). *Studies in word-association.* London: Heinemann.

Jung, C. (1928). *Contributions to analytical psychology.* New York: Harcourt.

Jung, C. (1933). *Psychological types.* New York: Harcourt.

Jung, C. (1953). *Collected works* (Vol 7): *Two essays on analytical psychology.* New York: Pantheon Press.

Jung, C. (1963). *Memories, dreams, reflections.* New York: Pantheon Press.

Kadushin, A. (1972). *The social work interview.* New York: Columbia University Press.

Kardiner, A. (1939). *The individual and his society.* New York: Columbia University Press.

Kardiner, A. (1945). *The psychological frontiers of society.* New York: Columbia University Press.

Kardiner, A. (1977). *My analysis with Freud: Reminiscences.* New York: W. W. Norton.

Karon, B. & Vandenbos, G. (1981). *Psychotherapy of schizophrenia: The treatment of choice.* New York: Jason Aronson.

Kaufman, I. (1958). Therapeutic considerations of the borderline personality structure. In H. Parad (Ed.), *Ego psychology and dynamic casework.* New York: Family Service Association of America.

Kernberg, O. (1973). *Borderline conditions and pathological narcissism.* New York: Jason Aronson.

Kernberg, O. (1993). The current status of psychoanalysis. *Journal of the American Psychoanalytic Association,* 41 (1), 45–62.

Kessel, L. & Hyman, H. (1933). The value of psychoanalysis as a therapeutic procedure. *Journal of the American Medical Association,* 101, 1612–1615.

Kissen, M. (1992). *Gender and psychoanalytic treatment.* New York: Brunner/Mazel.

Klein, D. & Wender, P. (1993). *Understanding depression: A complete guide to its diagnosis and treatment.* London: Oxford University Press.

Klein, M. (1932). *The psychoanalysis of children.* London: Hogarth Press.

Klein, M. & Riviere, J. (1937). *Love, hate and reparation.* London: Woolf and Hogarth Press.

Knight, R. (1953a). Borderline states. In R. Knight (Ed.), *Psychoanalytic psychiatry and psychology.* New York:

International Universities Press.

Knight, R. (1953b). An evaluation of psychotherapeutic techniques. In R. Knight (Ed.), *Psychoanalytic psychiatry and psychology*. New York: International Universities Press.

Kohut, H. (1971). *The analysis of the self*. New York: International Universities Press.

Kohut, H. (1977). *The restoration of the self*. New York: International Universities Press.

Kohut, H. (1978). *The search for the self*. New York: International Universities Press.

Kraepelin, E. (1917). *One hundred years of psychiatry*. New York: Citadel Press.

Lindon, J. (1966). Melanie Klein—Her view of the unconscious. In F. Alexander, S. Eisenstein, & M. Grotjahn (Eds.), *Psychoanalytic pioneers*. New York: Basic Books.

Malcolm, J. (1981). *Psychoanalysis: The impossible profession*. New York: Knopf.

Masson, J. (1984). *The assault on truth: Suppression of the seduction theory*. New York: Farrar, Straus & Giroux.

Masson, J. (1985). *The complete letters of Sigmund Freud to Wilhelm Fliess (1987–1904)*. Cambridge, MA: Harvard University Press.

Masson, J. (1990). *Final analysis: The making and unmaking of a psychoanalyst*. Reading, MA: Addison-Wesley Publishing Company.

May, M. (1991). Observations on countertransference, addiction, and treatability. In A. Smaldino (Ed.), *Psychoanalytic approaches to addiction*. New York: Brunner/Mazel.

Moore, B. & Fine, B. (1990). *Psychoanalytic terms and concepts*. New Haven, CT: Yale University Press.

Mullahy, P. (1948). *The contributions of Harry Stack Sullivan*. New York: Heritage House.

Munroe, R. (1955). *Schools of psychoanalytic thought*. New York: Dryden Press.

Orgler, H. (1963). *Alfred Adler: The man and his work*. New York: The New American Library.

Oring, E. (1984). *The Jokes of Sigmund Freud*. Philadelphia: University of Pennsylvania Press.

Pumpian-Mindlin, E. (1966). Anna Freud. In. F. Alexander, S. Eisenstein & M. Grotjahn (Eds.), *Psychoanalytic pioneers.* New York: Basic Books.

Rappaport, D. (1960). Structure of psychoanalytic theory: A systematizing attempt. *Psychological Issues* (Vol. 2, No. 2), Monograph No. 6. New York: International Universities Press.

Rank, O. (1924). *The trauma of birth.* Leipzig: International Psychoanalytic Verlag.

Rank, O. (1932). *Art and the artist.* New York: Alfred A. Knopf.

Rank, O. (1945). *Will therapy, truth and reality.* New York: Alfred A. Knopf.

Reich, W. (1948). *Character analysis.* New York: Orgone Press.

Reppen J. (1985). *Beyond Freud: A study of modern psychoanalytic theorists.* Hillsdale, NJ: The Analytic Press.

Roazen, P. (1975). *Freud and his followers.* New York: Alfred A. Knopf.

Sandler, J. Dare, C. & Holder, A. (1973). *The patient and the analyst.* New York: International Universities Press.

Schafer, R. (1983). *The analytic attitude.* New York: Basic Books.

Schafer, R. (1992). *Retelling a life.* New York: Basic Books.

Searles, H. (1978). Psychoanalytic therapy with the borderline adult. In J. Masterson (Ed.), *New perspectives on psychotherapy with the borderline adult.* New York: Brunner/Mazel.

Searles, H. (1979). *Countertransference and related subjects.* New York: International Universities Press.

Segal, H. (1964). *Introduction to the work of Melanie Klein.* New York: Basic Books.

Slakter, E. (1987). *Countertransference.* Northvale, NJ: Jason Aronson.

Smaldino, A. (1991). *Psychoanalytic approaches to addiction.* New York: Brunner/Mazel.

Socarides, C. (1978). *Homosexuality.* New York: Jason Aronson.

Spence, D. (1981). Psychoanalytic competence. *International Journal of Psychoanalysis, 62,* 113–124.

Stolorow, R. & Atwood, G. (1979). *Faces in a cloud: Subjectivity in personality theory.* Northvale, NJ: Jason Aronson.

Strean, H. (1970). *New approaches in child guidance.* Metuchen, NJ: Scarecrow Press.

Strean, H. (1975) *Personality theory and social work practice.* Metuchen, NJ: Scarecrow Press.

Strean, H. (1979). *Psychoanalytic theory and social work practice.* New York: The Free Press.

Strean, H. (1980). *The extramarital affair.* New York: The Free Press.

Strean, H. (1983). *The sexual dimension: A guide for the helping professional.* New York: The Free Press.

Strean, H. (1984). Homosexuality: A lifestyle, a civil rights issue or a psycho-social problem? *Current Issues in Psychoanalytic Practice,* (3), 35–47.

Strean, H. (1989). *The severed soul.* New York: St. Martin's Press.

Strean, H. (1990). *Resolving resistances in psychotherapy.* New York: Brunner/Mazel.

Strean, H. (1991a). *Behind the couch.* New York: Continuum.

Strean, H. (1991b). Colluding illusions among analytic candidates, their supervisors, and their patients: A major factor in some treatment impasses. *Psychoanalytic Psychology, 8,* 403–414.

Strean, H. (1993). *Resolving counterresistances in psychotherapy.* New York: Brunner/Mazel.

Strupp, H. (1977). *Psychotherapy for better or worse: The problem of negative effects.* New York: Jason Aronson.

Strupp, H. Fox, R. & Lesser, K. (1969). *Patients view their psychotherapy.* Baltimore: The Johns Hopkins Press.

Sullivan, H.S. (1931). The modified psychoanalytic treatment of schizophrenia. *American Journal of Psychiatry, 11,* 519–540.

Sullivan, H.S. (1947). *Conceptions of modern psychiatry.* Washington, DC: William Alanson White Institute.

Sullivan, H.S. (1953). *The interpersonal theory of psychiatry.* New York: W. W. Norton.

Sullivan, H.S. (1954). *The psychiatric interview.* New York: W. W. Norton.

Sulloway, F. (1979). *Freud: Biologist of the mind.* New York: Basic Books.

Taft, J. (1958). *Otto Rank.* New York: Julian Press.

Von Eckardt, B. (1985). Adolf Grunbaum: Psychoanalytic epistemology. In J. Reppen (Ed.), *Beyond Freud* (pp. 353–404). Hillsdale, NJ: The Analytic Press.

Wallerstein, R. (1986). *Forty-two lives in treatment.* New York: The Guilford Press.

Winnicott, D. (1958). *Collected papers.* New York: Basic Books.

Winnicott, D. (1965). *The maturational processes and the facilitating environment.* New York: International Universities Press.

Winnicott, D. (1971a). *Playing and reality.* New York: Basic Books.

Winnicott, D. (1971b). *Therapeutic consultations in child psychiatry.* New York: Basic Books.

Wollheim, R. (1977). *Philosophers on Freud: New evaluations.* Northvale, NJ: Jason Aronson.

Wolman, B. (1972). *Handbook of child psychoanalysis.* New York: Van Nostrand Reinhold Company.

Wyss, D. (1973). *Psychoanalytic schools.* Northvale, NJ: Jason Aronson.

INDEX

*(Note: Common psychoanalytic terms appear **boldface** throughout the index.)*

characteristics of (Kaufman),
83-84
Borderline personality organi-
zation, 85
Borderline states, 70, 83-85
Boring, E., 132
Brenner, C., 12, 77, 79, 91, 117
Briehl, Walter, 52
Bruke, Ernest, 5
Burlingham, Dorothy, 56

Cameron, N., 91, 92, 97
Catharsis, 5
Cathexes, 21
Causality, 35
Character, 50, 98
Character disorders, 95-97
Characterology, 51
Character traits, 96
Charcot, Jean-Martin, 5
Chicago Institute for Psycho-
analysis, 129
Child analysis, 63
Childhood, 48
Childhood and Society
(Erikson), 59
Children, diagnostic evaluation
of, 56-57
Clarification, 122, 124
Clark, R., 2, 3, 6
Clinical labels, and negative
countertransference, 78
Clinician (therapist), role of,
62-63
Cohesive self, 70
Colby, K., 135, 137
Collective unconscious, 36
Compensation, 29
Compensatory fantasy, 110-11

Complex(es), 35-36
constellating power of, 38-
39
Compromise formation, 76
Freud on, 76
symptom as, 75, 90-91
Compulsions, 90, 91
Condensation, 16
Conflict, 13, 49-50, 75-76
Conflict-free ego sphere, 53
Confrontation, 121, 123-24
Connective interpretation, 126
Conscience, 10
Consciousness, 15-17
Conversion hysteria, 92-93
Corsini, R., 2
Counterresistance, 115-17
Countertransference, 118-21
"Countertransference and Psy-
choanalytic Technique"
(Abend), 117
Counter-will, 33
Creative self, 30
Crises, 62
Culture, 23-24
*Current and Historical Perspec-
tives on the Borderline Pa-
tient* (Fine), 84-85
*Current Status of Psychoanaly-
sis, The* (Kernberg), 24-25
Dare, C., 125
Defense mechanisms, 13-15,
90, 103
ego and, 58
Defenses, 12-13
Denial, 15, 103
Depression, infantile, 64-65
Despair, 62
Determinism, 7

Maturation, 57
May, Mitchell, 93
Measurement problem, 137-38
Megalomania, 80
Memories, 31
Merger transference, 71
Metapsychology, 9, 22
Mirror transference, 71
Moods, alteration of, 81
Moore, B., 15, 40, 66, 67, 68, 69, 70, 82, 83, 85
Mother complex, 36
Mullahy, P., 45
Munroe, R., 45

Narcissism, 23, 81, 83
Narcissistic behavior disorders, 70
Narcissistic stage, 23
Narcissistic transference, 71
Negative countertransference, 120-21
  clinical labels and, 78
Negative therapeutic reaction, 104, 112-14
Neuroses, 34
  steps in, 80
Neurosis and Human Growth (Horney), 41
Neurotic needs, 43
Neurotic Personality of Our Time, The (Horney), 41
Neurotic solutions, 43-44
Neurotic symptoms, 31, 74
  Freud on, 76
Neurotic syndromes, conflict and, 49-50
Neurotic trends, 43
Neutralization, 54-55

New Introductory Lectures, The (Freud), 96
New York Psychoanalytic Institute, 41
Nuclear self, 69-70

Object love, 23
Object relatedness, lack of, 83
Object relations, 9
Observation, recording of, 136-37
"Observations on Countertransference, Addiction, and Treatability" (May), 93
Obsessions, 90, 91
Obsessive-compulsive neurotic, 91
Oedipus complex, 6, 19
  Klein on, 64
Omnipotence, 83, 84
Oral character, 96
Orality (Oral stage), 2, 18
Organic inferiority, 28-29
Organization, 57
Orgasm, function of, 50-51
Orgler, H., 27, 30
Oring, E., 3
Orgone, 51-52
Orientation in living, 48
Our Inner Conflicts (Horney), 41
Overdetermination, 87
Overemphasis on the past, 108-9
Overemphasis on the present, 107-8
Overidentification, 119